WINNING WAYS THROUGH CORPORATE GOVERNANCE

Also by Neville Bain

SUCCESSFUL MANAGEMENT

Winning Ways through Corporate Governance

Neville Bain

and

David Band

Foreword by Tim Melville-Ross

Coventry University

First published 1996 by
MACMILLAN PRESS LTD
Houndmills, Basingstoke, Hampshire RG21 6XS
and London
Companies and representatives
throughout the world

ISBN 0–333–66608–9

A catalogue record for this book is available
from the British Library.

This book is printed on paper suitable for recycling and
made from fully managed and sustained forest sources.

10   9   8   7   6   5   4   3   2   1
05   04   03   02   01   00   99   98   97   96

Copy-edited and typeset by Povey–Edmondson
Okehampton and Rochdale, England

Printed in Great Britain by
Mackays of Chatham PLC
Chatham, Kent

Coventry University

PO 633

13/2/97

Principles of good governance are first learnt in the home. My parents, and those of my wife Anni, provided warmth, encouragement and excellence in governance that is difficult to match. For my part, I dedicate this book to parents.

Neville Bain

For precisely the same reasons, I dedicate this book to another parent – Kim

David Band

Contents

List of Case Studies and Figures

Foreword

This is a remarkably good book. It strikes an effective balance between many conflicting objectives. For example, corporate governance can be so narrowly defined that it involves issues which are of no concern to anyone other than the company secretary. Alternatively, it can be so widely drawn that it covers the whole range of corporate activity. Neville Bain and David Band have succeeded in identifying the essence of good governance so that their book is of real value to all who need to take the subject seriously.

They have also succeeded in balancing the interests of both the business people and the academics who should read this book to appreciate the state of the art in corporate governance, and to understand what steps should be taken to improve the system.

No discussion on corporate governance – far less a serious work on the subject – can omit reference to the vexed question of directors' pay. But a fortunate balance has been struck here, too, recognising the seriousness of the subject, but also that it is only one element in a complex web that determines how the wealth-creation process can be most effectively handled. And in meeting the subject head-on, the authors ask the key question of how to get managers to modify their behaviour to reflect fully the best interests of shareholders. You will find the answers to that question here, too.

Another balance which the authors successfully strike, and which is the key challenge for every director, is that between enterprise and control. Is the director, especially the non-executive director, there to encourage the executive to create wealth in the most effective way, or, in the words of Sir Christopher Hogg, to spin 'endless webs of process around the executive on the assumption that evil will otherwise triumph'? The answer, of course, is that any effective director must contribute both to enterprise and control, and the more thoughtful will appreciate that the two objectives complement rather than conflict with each other. This will be all the more so should the individual concerned read this book, and in particular the chapter on the control environment, where the authors have managed to explain how effective control systems can be built in as an integral part of the process of running the company effectively. Much has been said, written and indeed implemented over the last few years on improving the control environment within which companies operate. There is, as the authors point out, an almost universal plea from the business community to allow what has been done a couple of years to settle down before yet further changes are brought in. It is very reassuring that this was almost the first point which Sir Ronald Hampel made when the new Committee on Corporate Governance set up under his chairmanship was first announced.

In writing about such a well-rounded book as this, it seems invidious to pick out just a few key themes. But it is my privilege to do just that, so I want to highlight what the authors have to say about improving relationships between institutions and boards of directors, improving boards themselves – especially their individual members – and improving communication.

My instinct as a businessman tells me that we could make great strides in improving the way companies operate, and perhaps more importantly the public perception of this, if we could find a way of strengthening relationships between institutional investors and companies in a constructive way which does not limit the freedom of action of companies to create wealth for the benefit of society as a whole. But the risk of taking this too far has to be recognised. As the authors say, it is possible to imagine situations in which investors would get far too deeply involved in corporate decision-making, and thus make directors and the companies they run significantly more risk-averse. But the authors' research shows that institutions place much value on regular contact with the management of a company and many would like to have more influence on the appointment of new directors.

In their conclusions, the authors advocate more relationship investing, whereby institutions actually appoint non-executive directors to boards to ensure that the companies concerned are more likely to perform in the best long-term interests of the shareholder in question, and thus, by extension, shareholders generally. A relatively small minority of those surveyed by the authors agree with this approach, but I cannot help feeling that the authors show considerable foresight in identifying this as an important future trend which will deliver significant benefits to institutions and companies alike if properly handled.

Turning to the effectiveness of boards themselves and individual directors, the reader will find much good sense in this book which shows how to determine not only whether a board is trying to do the right things, but is also doing them in the right way. As far as individual directors are concerned, I am afraid most of us assume we are now beyond the need for evaluation, and therefore for further training to overcome any shortcomings which might be identified as a result, or simply to keep us up to date with fast-changing modern conditions. Thankfully, this assumption falls away when directors stop to think, and it is interesting that a large majority of those questioned in the authors' research thought that compulsory training for all new directors, and top-up training periodically thereafter, was a good thing. The authors make the point themselves 'that most non-executive directors have time constraints and very few have been offered any formal training. While their knowledge-base will improve over time, we believe that regular, probably annual, training sessions are needed.' There is a duty on all of us involved in corporate governance to encourage more formal training for directors.

But, in a way, the heart of the matter is evaluation. It is vital that senior people should have sufficient humility to accept that, either as group or individually, they may not be performing to their maximum potential. Chapter 3 of the book asks the vital questions which must be answered to establish whether this is the case in individual board rooms, inevitably imposing a substantial burden on the chairman of the board as a result. What is more, any director who is wise enough to ask these questions of himself will find appendices to this important chapter against which he can measure his own capabilities and those of his board.

It would be wonderful if, as the authors would like to see, we could create conditions in which directors generally achieved such a high degree of professionalism, and moreover embarked consciously on a process of continuous learning, that it would be possible to create a register of directors which would carry a hallmark of excellence in this vital field. The suggestion in theirs, not mine, but what a vital role this would create for the Institute of Directors to perform!

And lastly, the authors have much wisdom to offer on the all-important question of communication. Once again, the word 'humility' comes to mind, in that companies, boards and individuals should be prepared to accept that what they are doing might be improved if they are prepared to expose it to critical scrutiny by others. Practising what they preach, the authors are communicating with great effectiveness in writing and publishing this excellent book.

TIM MELVILLE-ROSS
Institute of Directors

Preface

The motivation for writing this book is found in both authors' deeply held conviction that good governance is an essential element for any organisation that wishes to maximise its effectiveness. This is true in the public sector, in the commercial arena and in not-for-profit organisations. We are not alone in observing that in many cases companies or other organisations that perform badly are often poorly governed. Indeed, the key explanation for poor performance is often poor governance. This observation is not limited geographically for we can see many such examples from around the world, whether in developed or developing economies. Concern with good governance is not just limited to the free enterprise system. It is almost universal.

Governance is topical. In many countries, not least the United Kingdom, there are flurries of activity trying to deal with the symptoms rather than the cause. Equally, really significant contributions such as the Cadbury Report in the United Kingdom or the Working Group on Corporate Governance in the USA are devalued by the populist press or special interest groups.

There are genuine concerns in the community which pose hard questions:

- Why do we see widespread company failures when there is no apparent warning of failure in the company accounts?
- What is wrong when pension funds can mis-apply investments and lose so much value?
- Why do charities sometimes find that they have lost significant value off their investments and cannot meet their continuing obligations?
- How do we best deal with genuine concerns about the amount and make-up of rewards to the leaders of industry and at the same time maintain incentives to maximise performance?
- How can we improve board performance to maximise shareholders' long-term wealth but within a context that recognises the legitimate needs of other stakeholders?
- Do investors' and managers' objectives differ? Are some overly concerned with short-term performance while others are concerned with long-term value creation?

A review of recent press reports in many countries, but especially Britain, would leave the impression that corporate greed is rife and that directors have low ethical standards and limited competence. The major 'outrage' reflected in journalists' copy is to do with pay and associated benefits. This picture is distorted. While there are examples of excessive payments, of poor governance and inadequate performance of directors, this is not the norm. Further, such a focus does nothing to lift real performance standards in the corporate and wider non-profit sectors. This high noise level, seen in the press and mimicked by many politicians, trivialises the importance of governance.

We believe that putting corporate governance high on the agenda will add value to an organisation. It is important to restore trust between stakeholders and directors, between managers and boards and between large organisations and the communities of which they are part. We believe that over time trust will be restored if corporate governance is put high on the corporate agenda. For this reason, we decided to gather information from these various constituents in an endeavour to suggest the way forward to improve the governance of, and therefore the value produced by, such organisations.

We started by talking to key people in the community: business leaders, trade unions, decision-makers in about 50 institutions and senior representatives of the financial press. We used a questionnaire to provide a standard format which we have included in the appendix, but there was ample opportunity for freedom of views! The response was very high, reflecting the great interest in this broad area. This information provided our opening database which was limited to the United Kingdom. Needless to say, we also reviewed publications over the past five years or so on a worldwide basis to give a broader picture. On these bases, we then conducted many in-depth interviews with these same people. The key purpose here was to 'get behind' their views on contemporary governance issues and to tease out creative suggestions for resolving those issues.

The findings from this research are discussed in the opening chapter which also deals with other important scene-setting material. However, the findings are also reflected in other chapters and provided us with useful material when we considered the future direction for improving standards. While some would argue that increased legislation is the only sure way to guarantee a step change in standards, we take the view that it is more fruitful to create a climate of *desire* for improvement. The role of the board is crucial and the chairman's role is pivotal. Chapter 2 is therefore devoted solely to this. The board holds an absolutely pivotal role in ensuring that appropriate standards are laid down. It ensures that executives operate within the prescribed boundaries and to the agreed principles or standards laid down. But how should the board evaluate its own performance? We are clear that a board that consistently appraises its own performance performs much better, which is why we have included this as a separate topic in Chapter 3. Chapter 4 stays with the theme of the examination of the board by looking directly at the independent director and the investor. There is a good deal of evidence which suggests that non-executive directors are pivotal to the governance process yet they are not always well equipped to deal with the demands this brings. This chapter will be a helpful framework for non-executive directors who wish to objectively evaluate their contribution and how they can best influence the standards the company adheres to.

Even the best-laid plans of companies and their boards can face unexpected challenges. We have therefore included Dealing with the Unexpected as Chapter 5. Again, this will prove especially helpful to non-executive directors and a helpful checklist for experienced executive directors. The Control Environment included as Chapter 6 is very important as it goes to the heart of ensuring appropriate financial controls and measures. Audit committee members will find this a helpful summary of their role and will be challenged by the opportunities for managing the risk environment more effectively.

The scope of our work extends beyond the business sector. The principles outlined in the book are also applicable across non-profit organisations and government bodies and we have chosen to devote Chapter 7 to non-profit organisations. This gives the opportunity to dwell especially on the needs of this sector thus giving managers a perspective on governance that will improve their overall effectiveness.

Communication is key. Chapter 8 picks up on essential elements of communication to deal with this critical area of governance. The message may well be complex, it may even be to an agnostic audience, but it is a key task of all leaders to ensure the community is aware of the standards of governance.

The final chapter draws all of this together, offering a brief summary, some conclusions and challenges for the future, and in particular a proposed new model of corporate governance.

We believe that it is very timely to think pragmatically about governance and the best way forward. Objectivity is the starting point for better solutions in most fields of endeavour. Given the clamour of the media focused only on a narrow aspect – financial reward – a sense of balance is required. There is also an urgent need for leadership from thoughtful managers, community leaders and trade unionists to provide a sensible path forward. Regrettably, political parties are not providing this, and they attempt to narrow politically sensitive areas or to snipe at the edges with populist observations usually centred on the politics of envy. This is especially true in Britain. Our earnest hope is that sufficient thought, debate and action will render down these narrow, limiting activities and promote a more balanced, comprehensive response. If our book helps to achieve greater balance and some real movement on governance, we shall be pleased.

This book is a practical one which we believe should have a very wide appeal. It should be valuable to thoughtful directors and managers who wish to raise standards to improve performance. While there is a strong emphasis on the corporate sector for large and small companies alike, we believe that the same principles apply to the non-profit sector too. Those working in government will find the issues covered here helpful and relevant in any area where control is required, choices are needed and where different interest groups are involved. Of course, they will also gain a balanced insight into the important area of corporate governance that will be helpful in any debate in which they are involved. Lastly, we believe that there is much of value for those on advanced business programmes and we have included some helpful references to enable wider reading. We hope that this book is an enjoyable, easy read, written in a practical style that really adds to the debate.

We remain strongly of the view that directors around the world need to develop 'winning ways through integrity and good governance'.

NEVILLE BAIN
DAVID BAND

Acknowledgements

We have been warmly encouraged by the number of thoughtful people with whom we have spoken who believe in the positive value of a climate of good governance. At the same time, business people and academics alike have been bombarded with considering the impact of recommendations from bodies such as the Cadbury Committee, the Greenbury Committee and every changing requirements of the Accounting Standards Board. This continuing pressure and the trend towards regulation would normally turn off people from helping to research further in the general field of governance.

However, we were very heartened by the response, help and valuable insights provided by more than fifty busy people who gave freely of their time, giving a broad view of this topical area. We would like to thank these people for providing not only the valuable survey data for chapter one but for follow-up information that was further developed for later chapters. While these people remain anonymous by their choice, they also willingly provided input for the real life case studies included.

Tim Melville-Ross, Director-General of the Institute of Directors, has been a very valuable source of information. He also read through the entire draft, making valuable suggestions for improvement. We are especially grateful to Tim for providing the foreword and are very much encouraged that the Institute of Directors, under his leadership, places the governance issue high on the agenda. Clear evidence of this is seen in the Institute's Conference on Enterprise and Governance held in London at the end of October 1995.

Gill Nott, Chief Executive of ProShare, is a champion of the individual shareholder. She provided us with very interesting, helpful research material which helped provide balance to the views of the large institutions. In addition to this, Gill read through the manuscript providing insights and observations that we were pleased to received.

Simon Laffin, Finance Director of Safeway, provided insights, suggestions and the permission for the material on Safeway included in Chapter 6. Eric Samuelson and Sarah Sodeau of Coopers & Lybrand also provided invaluable help and perspective for Chapter 6. Equally, we would thank Peter Meinertzhagen, Carol Galley, Paul Myners and Sir

Alistair Grant for going through our draft work and providing numerous helpful suggestions. David Band wishes to acknowledge the contributions to his thinking made by the members of the Advanced Business Programme at the University of Otago – especially Joanne Esplin, Austin Groome, Chris Bates and Geoffrey Sullivan.

As we have used wider published work to provide a breadth of material for the reader, we have fully acknowledged this in the body of the work.

Both of the authors gratefully acknowledge the very real contribution in the production of our respective secretaries, Sue McBain and Kate Pegler who have kept control of the authors through their management of the process and professional input into the process which, without them, would have sunk into chaos!

The book would not have been possible save for the encouragement and support of our respective wives, Anni and Kim.

Many people have helped, guided and encouraged us which is both acknowledged and greatly appreciated.

However, the final work, along with any blemishes that we have failed to eradicate, is our responsibility. Our hope is that the final work is of value in raising the profile of governance standards in practice and is also an interesting, helpful read for the wide audience at which it is aimed.

NEVILLE BAIN
DAVID BAND

1 Setting the Scene

Concerns

There is considerable disquiet in the community which is calling into question present practices of governance. Depending upon one's perspective, the areas of discontent are clustered around the following:

- Low ethical and professional standards leading to poor performance and a loss of value in the various organisations.
- Double standards allowing practice to differ from stated ideals.
- Failures of commercial and non-profit organisations as a result of inadequate controls or unsatisfactory checks and balances.
- Inappropriate pursuit of short-term profit at the expense of either the longer-term or other stakeholders who are seriously disadvantaged.
- High rewards, apparently out of line with performance or with an appropriate peer group.
- A lack of transparency in remuneration practice.
- Tensions and frictions that arise from the different objectives of a management team which is separated from ownership.

This feeling of unease transcends many parts of the community at large. Within non-profit organisations many people are questioning the policies and controls that allow significant loss of value to occur, or in some cases for fraud to take place. Within the business community, other issues are being raised. For example:

- Does the community have expectations of the board of directors that are unrealistic and cannot be fulfilled?
- Non-executive directors now have a much higher level of responsibility and workload, making the role more onerous and time demands greater.
- There is an increasing trend to litigation, which means that directors may need to think first about protecting their position legally. This applies even more to advisors, especially auditors, who have to date been seen as deep pockets to be tapped at the first sign of trouble. These trends could have a significant impact on the *cost* of governance.

It is of course true that there is very thin evidence that is called upon to support claims that directors, acting as fat cats, rip off the community to make personal gain, or any of the other more racy suggestions peddled in the popular press. However, the issues raised under the heading of governance are important, and need to be addressed. They will go away neither with a change in government (indeed the reverse is more likely to be true!) nor of their own accord.

What is governance?

We need as a community to address the fundamental importance of governance. If proper standards are installed, the organisation can outperform its peer group. It will do this by having clear performance criteria, and creating an environment that will attract the best talent. It will benefit by being more broadly accepted and supported by the community at large. We do not underestimate the size of this task. No doubt our fellow citizens hold widely divergent views on the nature of governance. Even our own survey respondents, intimately and professionally involved with issues of governance, define the term in many ways. To give a flavour, governance is seen by some of our respondents in the following terms:

- 'Having an appropriate pay policy for senior people in industry.'
- 'Providing checks and balances to avoid the excesses of top bosses.'
- 'A set of procedures to protect the organisation from fraud or loss due to poor practice.'
- 'Providing checks on the management thus protecting shareholders.'
- 'Curbing the worst excesses of a greedy managing class.'
- 'Providing a control climate suitable to the organisation.'

While some of these responses may be considered less than pragmatic, or too narrow in definition, they do highlight some aspects of popular views of governance. We believe that the essence of governance is found in the relationships between the various participants in determining the direction and performance of organisations. The primary groups involved are the shareholders, the board of directors, and the management. However there are other players too. These include the customers, employees, suppliers, creditors and the community. We believe that the central concern of governance is to add value to as many organisational stakeholders as is practicable.

The central management focus, and underlying driver at boardroom level, is to see how value can best be created. To be fully successful, an organisation must add value at a faster pace than its peer groups if it is to deliver competitive advantage. This approach should be central to governance. The governance procedures put in place must be valuable over and above the cost of maintaining them. This may be achieved through risk reduction, loss avoidance or by creating an atmosphere that will attract the best talent, eager to work for that organisation. We are, therefore, of the view that winning ways through good governance are not just possible, but essential in today's competitive world.

Throughout this book we will illustrate that by having appropriate standards of governance the long-term performance is raised and total shareholder return is enhanced. This should not be seen as a soft option not to take hard decisions for the benefit of shareholders. Increasingly, variables are complex in our modern world requiring trade-offs to ensure long-term gain in shareholder value. While Adam Smith, in 1776, held the view that each person acting selfishly in his or her best interests also maximised value for society, this analogy breaks down today in the corporate sector. Any business that looks solely to the very short-run selfish maximisation of returns will destroy value in the medium to longer term.

The histories of western countries show that their early years were peppered with famous entrepreneurs who had the ideas, put up the risk capital, provided the management and took the rewards. This early model is well documented and understood, and continues to be a part of course work in economic theory. Over time, of course, we are aware of the separation of capital from management, especially with the growth of the joint stock company and the rise of a professional managerial class. It is this separation of risk capital from management that has exacerbated the governance crisis, because the motivation of the separate groups has tended to shift with the changed model. Therefore, one of the key questions which thoughtful managers and capital providers grapple with is how one can get managers to modify their natural behaviours, to fully reflect the best interests of shareholders. Put another way: how can we align the long-term interests of managers, directors and shareholders? This certainly is a live issue, which is developed further in Chapter 2 on 'The Role of the Board'.

We wish to provide a thoughtful yet practical insight into the governance issues currently under debate. We therefore enlisted the help and contribution of a number of different groups. Our first approach was to send a questionnaire to the top 50 financial institutions and to key respected figures in the financial press and another to the big accounting firms to get some input. A copy of the core questionnaire is included as an appendix. We have also been able to have follow-up discussions with a number of these respondents and with a broader group of people from the financial, business and political elements of the community.

These insights, presented in a structured way, provide valuable input on current concerns as well as giving clues to the way forward. Of course, this is not full-blooded quantitative research with a large enough sample to give statistical significance! This was not intended. Our claim is that the feedback is rich qualitatively and comes from an influential representation of the community in the United Kingdom. While our research is limited to the UK, we have supplemented this with a review of work undertaken in other countries. In total around 75 questionnaires were sent out to identified individuals of influence, and the return rate was more than 60 per cent.

Research findings

Investment policy

As expected, no institutions claimed to make investment decisions based on short-term considerations. While 8 per cent of respondents were prepared to buy and sell shares in companies based on current values, this was seen as a marginal exercise compared with their more fundamental investment decisions. The great majority of respondents saw their decisions as long term, based on fundamental analysis. Supplementing this was the view taken of the management ability within the companies being examined.

This is exactly in line with previously published research such as the 1994 study of a large committee chaired by Paul Myners entitled *Developing a Winning Partnership*. In this report, the idea that short-termism by institutional shareholders fundamentally impeded companies from taking long-term investments, was strongly repudiated. The report observed that 'pension funds and life insurers, which make up the bulk of UK institutional funds are both long term investors, seeking to match the long term nature of their liabilities. The National Association of Pension Funds has recently estimated that the average holding period for any given share in a pension fund portfolio is over 8 years.'

However, the nature of capital markets, in which market makers get their margin from taking a position in the market, will certainly result at the margin in a wider trading fluctuation of the short-term price of many companies' shares. This, of course, is a separate issue, and not a key point of influence for a company that could in any way reflect upon how it governs itself.

Communication and ability to influence

There is no doubt that the quality of the relationships between companies and their institutional shareholders is very important in setting the scene for strategic advances, or long-term investment decisions. Any company that ignores its shareholders until it needs their support, will receive a rude shock. Close communication is needed to ensure that there is a well-understood common ground of expectations of performance and direction. We were therefore not surprised that the institutions placed high value on their regular contact with the management of a company. This is not a novel finding. They would also like more opportunities to talk with the non-executive directors, especially the chairman. The previously mentioned study, *Developing a Winning Partnership*, observed that over the past ten years improvements had been made in communication between company management and shareholders. They also observed that more could be done, which is very much in line with the findings from our sample group.

We found that 88 per cent of the institutions surveyed were satisfied with the frequency of communication from companies but only two-thirds were happy with the quality. Questions dealing with the ability to influence companies on important issues such as strategy, current or medium-term performance, management performance, and the appointment of new directors produced a more mixed response. Many of those responding were conscious of the difficult borderline between influencing companies at critical times, and usurping the board's prime responsibility of driving the company performance. The division of capital and management causes some tension and grey areas.

The responses were as follows:

	Percentage who believe they have sufficient opportunity to influence %
Strategy	57
Management Performance	70
Appointment of New Directors	35

A number of institutions felt quite strongly that they would very much like to have a more positive influence on the appointment of new directors. Although any newly appointed director retires by rotation at the next annual general meeting, institutional shareholders would need to be very negatively disposed to vote against him or her at that time. Their preference is really to influence in advance, and to be taken into the chair's confidence earlier on.

While the responses we received showed a general satisfaction with the opportunity to influence, there remained concern that this influence was more weighted towards negative rather than proactive influence. Even amongst the institutions which felt they had plenty of opportunity to influence both management and the board where appropriate, some considered that this was largely in circumstances where performance was not satisfactory. However, most shareholders felt strongly that they should not and would not want to guide a company's management or usurp their role in any way when performance over time was broadly satisfactory. The ability to influence when the strategy is not working, when management is unsatisfactory or more generally when significant shareholder value is lost, was seen as sufficient in most circumstances.

The impact of non-executives

Whenever thoughtful people debate the importance of corporate governance, they place a high degree of importance on the role of non-executive directors. We feel strongly that the contribution of non-executive directors is critical in establishing, maintaining and improving standards of governance in organisations. We therefore dwelled upon the role of non-executives in our research. There is broad recognition that community expectations of non-executives is very high indeed, perhaps even requiring a contribution that is not achievable in the real world. We therefore should not have been surprised that only 21 per cent of respondents felt that non-executive directors contributed to a satisfactory standard. Many reasons were suggested for this. To give a flavour of the views, some of the opinions expressed were:

- 'Non-executives remain in the pocket of the chairman, and are not truly independent or add value.'
- 'There is no way that non-executives can provide a satisfactory challenge to the executive directors. They do not have the time to get behind the façade of presentations or the inclination to do the work required.'

- 'Non-executives do not have the training to do an effective job. They can only comment on what the executives choose to tell them.'
- 'The stock of capable people who are able and willing to take on the job of a non-executive director is quite limited.'
- 'You cannot expect to get high quality non-executive directors while companies continue to pay inadequate directors' fees.'
- 'They want to give the benefit of their experience and to maximise their contributions to the companies they serve. They are conscious of their joint responsibilities as a director, but also the point of difference they must bring as a non-executive director, who must challenge the executive over a wide front whenever they feel it is appropriate to do so. This relative schizophrenia, while challenging, is not an inhibitor to a harmonious board where the chair is capable and sets up the appropriate boardroom culture.'

Innovations

We next asked the respondents which, if any, of the following suggestions they would support as an innovation to improve governance:

		Percentage agreeing %
1.	The creation of a professional set of non-executive directors appointed by institutional shareholders.	18
2.	Abandoning appointments of directors where there is a cross-holding of influence through common cross-directorships.	83
3.	Restricting individual non-executive directorships to three where that director already has executive responsibilities; to six in other cases.	95
4.	Recognising in statute that non-executive directors have a dual role as a legal director and to provide checks and balances on the executive.	82
5.	Widening the scope and depth of the audit committee to require it to have a more proactive role, especially in areas of internal control, balancing risk and return.	76

		Percentage agreeing %
6.	Compulsory training for all new directors to a minimum level including a period of orientation to the new company and 'top up' training for a period of 5 hours a year for all.	65
7.	Required consultation by management with the top 20 institutional shareholders such matters as:	
	• significant changes in strategy	50
	• changes to the board	47
	• remunerations programmes for directors	61
8.	Rotating audit firms every, say, 4 years.	41

Key messages

What key messages do we glean from these returns? First, there is a genuine desire of both the boards and institutions to have better quality communication, and to work more effectively together. In general, while the frequency of communication is broadly satisfactory, the quality is not. Companies will therefore need to review how they can improve in this area, and institutions need to be more forthcoming about their concerns. The concept of the company presenting and the institutions simply asking questions is not the best model for the future; indeed, it is unacceptable.

Second, recognising the greater demands placed on non-executive directors, there was support for a limit to the number of directorships (ranging from 3 to 7) that should be held by one person. In general, the role of non-executive directors caused a good deal of debate, as there is a general consensus that:

- The quality is not high enough, and more training is desirable.
- There is in reality a distinction between the role expected of a non-executive director compared with a director in general. This is not recognised in law, except perhaps in Australia.
- The different expectations of a non-executive director is a troublesome issue and potentially divisive.

Third, institutions would like a greater say on a few key issues, especially new board appointments, or on remuneration policy when new, perhaps adventurous, proposals are made. They dislike 'voting down' proposed issues at formal meetings. However, there is growing evidence that institutions will increasingly vote their shares on key issues and use proxies more widely.

Fourth, the role of the audit committee is very much at central stage. There is a strong desire to improve its scope and effectiveness, but there were no concrete proposals on how this should be effected.

Finally, only 41 per cent wanted to see audit firms regularly rotated, say every 4 years. However in our discussions there was a good deal of unease expressed about auditor–client relationship. At present, in the UK, one audit partner can remain in place for 7 years, and hand over to a colleague who has been working with him on that audit. All this in an environment where the firm will routinely receive other accounting work from the company. Justice must not only be done, it must be seen to be done.

Areas for improvement

Each respondent was invited to make one suggestion that would improve current standards of governance. We have grouped the responses under the following broad headings, which have been listed in order of frequency mentioned:

		%
1.	A need to have a better understanding of strategy	30
2.	A desire to influence new board appointments in advance of the decision	23
3.	An opportunity to have a separate discussion with the non-executive directors alone	15
4.	Create an annual forum for institutions to make their views known to the board (executive and non-executive directors)	15
5.	A better understanding of the business levers that influence performance	9
6.	More legislation to ensure higher standards of governance	8

Further insights into the top of mind agenda of institutions can also be found from the responses to the questions posed on how board–shareholder relations could be improved. This elicited areas where there is at present a high noise level, and boards are now seen to be responding effectively. Many replies prefaced their views with the observation that over recent years improvements have been made. A few volunteered that in general they were happy enough with the current situation, but as is always the case in any field there is room for improvement. We were also reminded that institutions have their own 'shareholder groups' whom they represent. They may be small policyholders, or large pension funds who have their funds professionally managed. 'Companies need to be much more sensitive to their concerns', advised one of the biggest institutions. 'If they thought more about this then company communication and behaviour may well be modified.'

Top of the list for current concern was pay packets of senior executives, and how these were linked to performance. 'The links need to be more clearly understood, and there must be greater transparency' was a typical reply. Next, the question of communication quality was raised. This broad area covered (again) the request for a meeting with non-executive directors and better strategic information on a regular – say, annual – basis. A few thought quarterly reporting would help, but many felt that the annual reports and annual general meetings were 'missed opportunities'.

We were not surprised by the weight of concern around the question of pay packets, given the high media profile of this topic, and given the weight of other supporting research. The William M. Mercer Ltd research published on 27 September 1995 reported on its survey of institutional investors' reactions to the 1995 report of a study group on Directors' Remuneration which was chaired by Sir Richard Greenbury (Greenbury Report). Ninety-three per cent of their replies supported full disclosure of remuneration policy and 80 per cent of replies believed that 'fuller disclosure will help curb excesses in executive pay'. Further, 76 per cent wanted to have the opportunity to vote on all long term incentive plans, and there was much evidence that institutions are prepared to be more proactive in using their votes to influence the make-up of remuneration committees, or on the reappointment of directors where the length of employment was deemed to be excessive. The other related area of common ground is that 92 per cent of institutions believed that remuneration plans should be used as a way of building up an executive shareholding in the company concerned.

Individual shareholders

The popular image of the smaller, individual shareholder is that of the free-loader at annual meetings looking for the complimentary food, drink and other goodies. They often like to make points at meetings, especially of a personal nature or on topical issues such as remuneration. This view is too narrow, although it is one that is held by many company chairmen! There are many small shareholders who have placed their investments in the hands of fund managers or through nominees, and in the great majority of cases they have given up any direct say or influence. It is a matter of some frustration to a number of these shareholders that their views are really seldom registered. ProShare has endeavoured to address this issue, and they too helped provide material for us.

In the words of Gill Nott, Chief Executive, 'Companies should not distinguish between their shareholder base or give preference to larger shareholders.' She believes that someone needs to speak out for small shareholders, whether it is in providing a level playing field of communication or in making documents easier to read by ordinary people.

This is not just a British phenomenon as small shareholders in a number of countries are banding together to form pressure groups to ensure their voice is heard. As an example, in France, two active groups are pressing for greater accountability from directors towards the small shareholder. These two groups, ADAMS (the Association for the Defence for Minority Shareholders) and ANAF (the National Association of French Shareholders) are showing signs of working together to have their interest groups' views put more forcibly. Ms Collette Neuville, who is head of ADAMS, was, for example, reported in the *Financial Times* on 14 August 1995 as saying 'We have to reverse the order of things so that companies and directors operate in the interests of shareholders, not the other way around.' The pressure group in France has a strong base given the relatively higher proportion of a company's shareholding that is held by individual shareholders.

There is then a feeling amongst a number of private investors that they are very much subjugated to the needs of the large shareholders who get the first opportunity to gain new insights or new information through regular briefings. Again, Gill Nott observes that 'increasingly, small shareholders feel like second class citizens for they are short-changed in the provision of information or in consultation. Any widening of the gap that currently exists by providing greater consultation with large shareholders will be resented.' While we can understand these feelings, it is more problematic to find an appropriate way forward that is time effective for the company.

When analysts and institutions are briefed, there is no price sensitive information passed on at such briefing meetings. Indeed, even if there is a hint of new information being provided, a synopsis of this is given to the Stock Exchange not later than the commencement of the meeting. However, this does not stop share price movement based on market-makers taking a position.

How can the thoughtful company bridge the gap between differing expectations and the practice of today? There are a number of ways in which improvements in communication with individual shareholders can be made. These include:

- Better quality annual reports or, better still, précis reports in simple English that are more digestible to smaller shareholders. This is equally true for the interim results or quarterly results if applicable.
- The annual general meeting could be made much more of an information update with less emphasis on formal business. One private investor we spoke with put it this way: 'If the AGM became a focus for sharing real information on strategy, outlook and in-depth reviews of parts of the group, this would be extremely helpful. It would make a change from the unseemly gallop through formal business to close the meeting before too many awkward (or sometimes trivial) questions are asked'.
- Open days at company sites for all shareholders to see a review of operations and to cover some of the material presented to analysts. ProShare, for example, does arrange for occasional briefings of individual shareholders with a number of companies. This provides a forum to talk about the company, its strategy and plans.

While there are improvements that companies can make in communication with small shareholders, it will be difficult to meet their full expectations. Management of companies must achieve the returns required by shareholders and, given the time constraints, they will tend to allocate more to the shareholders with greater clout and who are in the top 20 or 30 shareholders. However, more sensitivity or consideration of the smaller shareholders will no doubt generate improvements.

The institutions

Individuals are often the final owners of institutions through life policies, pension plans or equity-based savings plans. There is a deep question of how those major institutions can reflect in their behaviour the views of the myriad of individuals. In reality, there is little chance of providing any sensible forum for influence, which may be just as well. The body concerned has to focus on maximising long term value for all its members. However, the institutions need to have codes of practice which will cover their own governance. There will be a much greater readiness to listen to the views of an institution that practises high standards of governance for itself.

ProShare were asked how greater sensitivity to the needs of institutions' constituents could be put into practice. Clearly, there is no case for reflecting sectional interests. Gill Nott felt that 'Bodies such as the National Association of Pension Funds or the Association of British Insurers need to set standards and to remind their respective membership that institutions are the custodians of *their* owners, that is, the small investors and should do more to reflect their views.'

The rights of small shareholders are diminished in a number of ways when their holdings are through nominees. Quite often these shareholders are compulsorily passive as they do not directly receive information from the company. They find it difficult or cumbersome to attend the public meetings, as they are not registered shareholders and cannot vote.

ProShare, who believe strongly in the practice of equal treatment of *all* shareholders, wish to see a greater protection of shareholder rights. The ProShare nominee code issued in August 1995 is an attempt to gain acceptance of the basic rights of small shareholders who account for 20 per cent of the average share register. This code covers:

- Provision of company information, of any company perks, rights to attend and vote at meetings (including using a proxy vote).
- Information on the costs of using nominees.
- Safeguarding shares or other assets held for the individual.

While these may seem to be simple or obvious requests, they have not been universally accepted at this time. In part, some of this is due to administrative cost and difficulty, and in other cases, especially discretionary portfolios, the managers wish to retain flexibility of operation for themselves. However, there is no doubt that the issues raised are important ones which can influence an individual's method of saving or investment. Failure to meet reasonable requests may further reduce the individual shareholder's appetite for equity, thus increasing the institutions' overall shareholding percentage. This raises a wider philosophical question about what shareholder base is in the best interests of society and of the company. Do we want a broad balance or not? Perhaps this question is not the central focus of the pragmatic manager. Given the structure of shareholdings today, the total shareholder base needs to be appropriately and cost-effectively serviced.

A question of pay

There is no doubt that this is both an emotive and sensitive issue. As Sir Richard Greenbury told us, 'The question of pay and rations was, to my surprise, a much more sensitive issue than the Report of the Cadbury Committee on the Financial Aspects of Corporate Governance.' There is a genuine public grievance which, while inflamed by the media, is not just an issue whipped up to sell copy. Many people, according to the evidence we have, like to see the financial success of pop stars, sports personalities and the like but are envious of others. The public at large is also remarkably silent on the high income of self-employed professionals, merchant bankers and TV presenters. However, in the corporate arena there is a deep suspicion amongst a section of the community that there is a deal of collusion at board level in the fixing of remuneration.

Interestingly enough, according to ProShare, the question of levels of remuneration for directors does not rank amongst the most important items on the small shareholder's agenda. Naturally enough, in blatant cases of excess or where poor communication does not make the link between reward and performance obvious, there will be questions asked. Gill Nott comments, 'Most of the individual shareholders are not concerned about high pay per se. They want to see management highly rewarded for being effective. Shareholders are concerned about their bottom line – how well the company has done and how this is reflected in shareholder return.' This view is well documented in the private research undertaken for the submissions to Greenbury and which was made available to us.

The focus on pay that has been publicly debated to date has largely centred around salaries, bonuses, long-term incentive plans and share options. The rewards from this cocktail of earnings opportunities are considered alongside the progress of the company and the progress of its peer group. So far, the question of the cost to the company of pension contributions of senior executives has escaped all but a passing reference. In part, this is due to the fact that there is no universally agreed way of showing the individual costs. This is currently being addressed by the actuaries following the Greenbury Report. To illustrate the issue, a company with a pension holiday and with directors included in the company scheme will show zero contribution even though the underlying actuarial cost could vary from 15 per cent of salary to 70 per cent in extreme cases. Where the director was appointed after 1989 when the Conservative government capped salaries for pension purposes at £75,000 plus inflation (now £78,600 p.a.), the full costs are usually shown.

As an example, in Coats Viyella Plc's annual report, the Chief Executive's pension contribution is shown as averaging 40 per cent of salary in the last two years as he joined in 1990. The remaining directors show a nil contribution as the company pension fund is in substantial surplus and a pension contribution holiday is in place.

This issue, raised by Greenbury, will become a talking point in the next couple of years as the real costs become more transparent. Further, inevitably, there will be a public debate amongst actuaries, remuneration consultants and companies on the most appropriate way to provide the information. This is likely to inflame opinion once again.

Following on from the Greenbury recommendations, which for convenience we have precised in Figure 1.1, William M. Mercer carried out a brief survey of institutions to ascertain their attitudes to the report. This was published on 27 September 1995.

In summary, its survey results generally showed that the institutions support the Greenbury recommended actions but were not very proactive on these issues. Currently, many institutions are reviewing their policy and change is expected. Figure 1.2 summarises some of the main points from the William Mercer survey which are relevant to our research.

Summary

Common threads

What are the common threads that run through the evidence that we have gleaned from the research undertaken by ourselves and others? In summary, these are:

- **Code of Best Practice** lists a number of recommendations which should be complied with and any areas of non-compliance should be explicitly explained and justified.

   It recommends that the Stock Exchange make compliance with the code mandatory for listed companies.

- **Remuneration Committee**. The committee reached a number of important conclusions which strengthen the role and increase the importance of the committee.

   (i)   The committee should be made up exclusively of non-executive directors and should determine the company's overall policy on remuneration including salary, bonus, other incentives and pensions.

   (ii) The committee must be directly accountable to shareholders which will include attendance at the AGM and appropriate reporting in the annual report.

   (iii) The committee should have access to appropriate professional advice and consult the company chairman and chief executive.

- **Disclosure and Approval Provisions**

   (i)   A formal annual statement should be made each year setting out the remuneration policy and full details of the remuneration package of individual directors. This includes full details of salary incentives and pensions.

   (ii) Contract terms should be disclosed for directors. Terms in excess of one year are discouraged.

   (iii) New long-term incentive plans should be approved by shareholders.

- **Remuneration Policy**. The report asks that the policy should attract, retain and motivate directors of the required quality in the long-term interests of the company. Packages should be based on relevant, stretching criteria designed to enhance the business. Incentives should be long term using company shares which directors should be encouraged to retain.

- **Service Contracts and Compensation**. In compensating directors for departure on early termination of their contracts, account should be taken of the reasons for departure. A tough stance on compensation for poor performance should be taken. Consideration should be given to paying compensation in instalments to allow an opportunity to reduce or end them when new employment is found by the director.

Figure 1.1   Précis of Greenbury recommendations

1. 50% think that Greenbury has addressed the issues it was set up for.
2. 57% of institutions express a view on remuneration of companies to their clients or companies.
3. 63% of institutions do not solicit input from their client when deciding how to vote or tell their clients how to vote.
4. 70% will check that companies they invest in have complied with the Greenbury Code.
5. 93% want the remuneration committee to make a full disclosure on executive remuneration and believe it is important to have a representative at the AGM.
6. 80% believe that a fuller disclosure will help to curb excesses in executive pay.
7. 52% will investigate the make-up of the remuneration committee and vote against a non-executive director's re-election if he or she is considered to be unsuitable (e.g. cross-directorships).
8. 64% will not routinely vote against directors' service contracts in excess of one year.
9. 76% welcome the opportunity to vote on all long term incentive plans.
10. 97% believe that remuneration plans should concentrate more on building up an executive shareholding in the company.
11. 80% believe that executive pay issues should be influenced by pay and employment conditions elsewhere in the company.

SOURCE: Derived from 'The Survey of the Institutional Investors on the Greenbury Report', William M. Mercer, September 1995.

Figure 1.2 Summary of findings from survey of institutions

1. There is clear agreement that the quality of relationships between companies and their shareholders is very important.
2. Institutions and companies have a strong incentive to bridge any gap between each other and improve mutual understanding.
3. Institutions would like an opportunity to influence new director appointments before these are made. They do not want directors to represent any special interest groups, but wish to influence the quality and independence of appointments. However, this increased influence is strongly resisted by ProShare acting on behalf of smaller, individual shareholders.

4. Communications with shareholders can be further improved, especially in relation to:

   - outlining strategy
   - remuneration policy
   - board changes
   - better quality direct communication through annual reports and interim reports
   - providing higher quality information at annual general meetings.

5. Non-executive directors are important and will be a more powerful influence for governance in the future. They need to be truly independent, better trained and better rewarded, especially where they also chair the critical committees of remuneration and audit.
6. The role of the audit committee can usefully be broadened to provide a greater degree of good governance on financial issues.
7. Remuneration of top executives is a matter of genuine concern. The answer, however, is not to provide blanket restrictions, as most shareholders want to provide incentives and reward well for good performance.
8. Greater transparency in remuneration policy and practice is essential. The challenge is to provide this in a concise way without creating information overload.
9. A number of respondents suggested that we need a settling-down period of at least a couple of years to see how Cadbury and Greenbury influence actual practice.

Unresolved issues

Companies need to be even-handed with quality, timely information for all of their shareholder base. Small shareholders, according to ProShare, believe they are not getting this at present because of the preoccupation of companies with the 80 per cent shareholder base of institutions. A practical solution needs to be found to provide some succour to the smaller groups. This may be found in better quality communication, including special printed matter or videos on the theme of 'This is your company', site visits and so on. The annual general meeting largely remains a lost opportunity.

The question of how to show the costs of pensions of senior people in a company is not yet resolved. This is a sensitive area that requires careful evaluation and communication to avoid the counter-productive public point scoring of sectional groups in the community. What the media and other sectional interests have ignored, in whipping up a frenzy on this issue, is that vast numbers of Britons are company owners. Millions of our fellow citizens have a direct interest in good practice being observed in this area. The issue here should not be envy. It should be about furthering the interests, as shareholders, of these citizens.

Institutions have not fully resolved their role and interface with the companies they invest in. They need to have a more common approach on the areas it is appropriate for them to influence and to decide how this is best done. At the moment there are as many approaches as institutions.

Topics to be addressed further

Arising from these findings we believe that there are some important topics that need to be further addressed. We believe that the most important are:

- The role of the board
- The role of the non-executive director
- How the audit committee can be improved in scope and performance
- The control environment, and managing business risks
- How to further improve mutual understanding and communication between shareholder and the board.

These will be addressed in more detail in later chapters of the book. The one fundamental point that must always override all decisions is that of value creation. The board and each of its members have a responsibility to create value for the shareholders over the long term. This prime aim will influence all that they do, and will affect how they respond to the community concerns that are raised from time to time.

2   The Role of the Board

Good governance is the board's duty. It is responsible for setting standards and ensuring that the company achieves them. To put this into context, we will need to look in totality at the role of the board and to match this against current community expectations. We will see a gap between these expectations and current practice. The organisation and composition of the board will influence its effectiveness and, perhaps more than anything else, the chairman will have a major impact.

Duties of the board

The board is, of course, accountable to the shareholders. They have appointed the directors to act for shareholders' greater good. Historically, shareholders may well have rubber-stamped appointments but in today's climate this is no longer universally true. There are plenty of examples of institutional shareholders using their franchise to vote against directors or more usually to lobby against appointments seen to be unsatisfactory. This more proactive approach may well be used when issues are at stake or where a company has drifted and needs strong leadership to bring it back on track. However, looking forward, leading institutions tell us of their increasing desire to be consulted about changes to the board. This is dealt with in more depth in Chapter 1. This trend of increased interest in board appointments is also something that excites the interest of a growing number of smaller, individual shareholders at annual general meetings. They will, often noisily, draw attention to their displeasure over directors' actions by speaking out and voting against directors who have retired by rotation and seek re-election.

However, the board has an amalgam of functions which can be summarised as follows:

- The board is the representative of the shareholders to ensure the company has clear goals and to measure progress against those goals.
- The board will agree the strategy and the resources to achieve it.

21

- The chief executive is appointed by the board which monitors his or her performance and that of the senior management team.
- Because of the absolute importance of the human resource to achieve the agreed strategy, the board must annually review succession and management development plans.
- The board will need to set down and monitor the operating climate in the company through a statement of values that describes the character of the company and policies that reflect those values.

The position is made more complex because these functions must be carried out whilst complying with legal obligations and the social responsibilities of good citizenship. Then, for good measure, every company knows that it disregards other stakeholders – employees, customers, suppliers, governments and local communities – at its real peril. Despite the complexities, the board must choose the external standards to which the organisation must respond, recognising not only its primary accountability to shareholders but its wider role with the broader group of stakeholders. In setting out their primary functions, the best boards recognise that they, like the managers in the company, need to add value and to define where they can make the best contribution.

Expectations

There are diverse expectations of a board and its directors that are held by different groups in society. First, the shareholders expect the board to act in their best interests, providing acceptable total shareholder returns when compared with peer groups or 'competitors' for shareholders' money. They often exert short term pressures too, requiring the company to deliver regular increases in share price or dividends despite the challenges of economic circumstance.

Second, governments are increasingly endeavouring to transfer more welfare tasks to the private sector, especially if this provides a saving in government expenditure or transfers a thorny problem to the private sector. Governments therefore have an expectation that companies will provide these services as part of their 'good citizenship' or at least they can be forced to undertake duties on government's behalf without too much of a backlash. Examples of the latter could be collection of tax from employees or self-assessment of tax.

Third, employees have historically often held the view that they held a 'job for life'. In many industries this was indeed the case. This has been shattered in the last decade. Now, the claims are for improved pay and conditions and in many cases a concern to maintain or grow levels of employment. This sectional expectation may not be possible in a competitive world.

Fourth, customers and suppliers have increasingly moved towards partnership relationships that provide new challenges for a board's freedom of action or the timing of implementation of agreed actions.

Fifth, the community at large has an economic interest in a company's operation through the employment created, services used and funds made available through local government or community involvement. This is especially true in industries that have built facilities, often in fairly remote areas, to secure good local employment at affordable rates of pay but where few alternative employment opportunities exist. Increasingly, there is an added expectation that especially the management of these local operations will be more greatly involved in local affairs such as charities, churches, school committees and local governments.

Finally, the public at large has a wide variety of items to hold the board accountable for. These are usually well publicised by the media and include:

- limiting senior executives' compensation
- full environmental protection
- avoidance of fraud within the company
- hiring and firing the key executives
- caring for employees

The point is that expectations placed on the board are often conflicting, unrealistic or based on a false understanding of responsibility. There is then a role of communication by the business community at large that needs to be taken up. However, there is also a growing feeling that the importance, complexity and scale of organisational activity is such that changes to governance are desirable and that the topic of corporate governance will be important over at least the next decade.

The members of the working party on corporate governance in the United States reported their 'New Compact for Owners and Directors' in the *Harvard Business Review* (July–August 1991). They counselled shareholders to recognise that only one legitimate goal for shareholders is appropriate, namely ongoing prosperity for all shareholders. They should not therefore pressure companies to pursue different goals that might have some other attraction to a few. Therefore, shareholders should not act in ways that would frustrate or detract from the ongoing prosperity of that company. We believe that this is a fundamental point that needs to be acknowledged by all groups of shareholders. Directors have a responsibility to *all* shareholders whether they are institutions, charities or individual investors.

Management of the board

Any top body needs to have goals and some basic rules that it uses in its day-to-day governance. The board is no exception to this principle. In most free enterprise countries there is broad agreement that the following areas of concern are important in management of the board. They are:

1. The board must agree how it will manage itself. This will include its composition, its agenda, process and performance.
2. It will have a clear understanding of directors' terms of tenure and how new appointees are nominated and chosen.
3. There will be a process to monitor the chief executive and his or her senior colleagues which will involve the chairman and non-executive outside directors alone.
4. The chairman will ensure that there is a periodic opportunity to review the functioning of the board.
5. There must be freedom for the outside directors to meet with inside directors, individually or collectively. This will include information-seeking, individual discussion on a topic of interest or socially to build up the two-way benefits of networking.
6. Either through committees or direct involvement, there must be an appropriate opportunity to review compensation plans, succession plans, strategy and issues of internal control.

The chairman

One of the less fruitful debates is to set down the case for and against a chairman being executive or non-executive or the case for full-time or part-time chairmen. Each company will have its own needs which will make the search for the appropriate role easier. Our own view is that, in almost all circumstances, it is proper to separate the role of chairman from chief executive in the interests of providing checks and balances.

Perhaps in the United Kingdom the great majority of companies expect the chief executive to be the one in whom the executive authority of the company is vested. What is absolutely certain is that there needs to be a clear understanding of whether the chairman or chief executive is directly accountable for the formulation and implementation of strategy and is also directly accountable for the results. Of course, in the final analysis the board will be finally responsible for strategy but the initiator of that will normally be the chief executive. The exception would be where the chairman is in a full-time executive role.

The chairman is, without doubt, the leader of the board and therefore must set the standards required from board colleagues. He or she must provide the required leadership by following an appropriate agenda. The contribution of the chairman will ultimately determine the board's effectiveness. Style may vary but standards must remain high.

There is both an internal and an external role for the chairman. So far, we have dwelt on the internal role. Externally, the chairman is often seen as the responsible person who ensures that appropriate standards are in place and who is accountable publicly in the event of a failure. It is perhaps ironic that, in the case of a failure down the executive line, it is the chairman who is held publicly accountable. Some see this challenge of accountability in terms of needing to be seen to pass appropriate policies or limiting the risk of potential legal claims by calling for regular reports. Others, more thoughtfully, understand that they need not only to install policies at the board but also to follow up to see that they are receiving much more than lip-service down the line.

As the chairman is also the link between board and shareholders, he or she needs to be satisfied with the corporate reporting to them. This will embrace the interim and annual results, the annual report, the annual general meeting and periodic reports on special occasions such as during takeovers. Reporting of results to analysts and institutions is also an important event where the chairman's presence and involvement is expected. The presentation requires orchestration to yield the best results with a clear slot for the chairman and a seamless transfer to the chief executive and finance director who will also be taking part. A chairman must therefore:

- be a strong leader
- have the intellectual capacity to deal with complexity and multi-dimensional issues
- be a capable communicator
- have both the energy and the time to get around the company and see the key executives in action on their own turf.

Matters reserved for the board

The Cadbury Committee, reporting on the financial aspects of corporate governance, recommended that the board should have a formal schedule of matters reserved for its decision, thus ensuring that the direction and control of the company is firmly in its hands. The Committee envisaged that the schedule would include at least:

1. Acquisition and disposal of assets of the company or its subsidiaries that are material to the company.
2. Investments, capital projects, authority levels, treasury policies and risk management policies. The board would lay down rules to determine materiality and agree procedures to be followed.

Almost all major companies in the United Kingdom now report full compliance against the recommendations of the Cadbury Committee. Some have questioned whether the focus of activity has been on accommodating the form while making little change to the practical lifting of good standards of governance. For example, the Northern Foods 1993 annual report, in welcoming the Cadbury Report, observed that 'there is a danger . . . that form becomes more important than practice'.

We have had the opportunity to view a number of boards' documentation to see those items reserved for the board and to observe how agendas have changed. The pattern is mixed, for at one end are companies that have formalised items for the board yet where the agenda and modus operandi has scarcely changed. In others, change is clear and the best companies have shown thoughtfulness in deciding those items reserved for the board with a change to the agenda emphasis.

We have included as Figure 2.1 a copy of the relevant board minute of a FTSE 50 company which has taken this topic seriously and has, over a number of areas, significantly improved its governance. This is followed with an example that is from a FTSE 100 company which is much briefer and is included as Figure 2.2. Despite this statement's brevity, this second company has made great strides in genuinely changing from one where governance was seldom considered to one where it is high on the agenda. This company has benefited from this changed approach in being more highly rated by investors, more trusted by analysts and more able to recruit good people.

Figure 2.1

Matters Reserved for Consideration by the Board

In order to ensure effective control over the affairs of the business, it was suggested that certain items of business and/or areas for consideration/authorisation be reserved for review/approval by the Board. After consideration

IT WAS RESOLVED THAT

consideration and/or decisions in relation to the undernoted items/matters be reserved for the collective decision of the Board or, where appropriate, a Committee of the Board and not delegated to individual Directors or executives:

Companies Act Requirements

1. Approval of interim and final financial statements.
2. Approval of an interim dividend and recommendation of the final dividend.
3. Approval of any significant change in accounting policies or practices.
4. Appointment or removal of the Company Secretary.
5. Remuneration of auditors (where, as is usual, shareholders have delegated this power to the board) and recommendations for appointment or removal of auditors.

Stock Exchange

1. Approval of all circulars and listing particulars (and approval of routine documents such as periodic circulars re scrip dividend procedures).
2. Approval of press releases concerning significant matters decided by the Board.

Management

1. Approval of the group's commercial strategy.
2. Approval of the group's Annual Operating Budget.
3. Approval of the group's Annual Capital Expenditure Plan.
4. Changes relating to the group's capital structure or its status as a plc.
5. Terms and conditions of employment of Directors and their service agreements.
6. Major changes to the group's management and control structure.

Figure 2.1 continued overleaf

Figure 2.1 continued

Board Membership and Board Committees

1. Board appointments and removals.
2. Terms of reference, if any, of chairman, deputy/vice chairman, chief executive and other executive Directors.
3. Terms of reference and membership of board committees.

Cadbury Recommendations

1. Major capital projects. (Projects in excess of £30m).
2. Material contracts of the Company (or any subsidiary) in the ordinary course of business, e.g. bank borrowing in excess of £25m.
3. Contracts of the Company (or any subsidiary) not in the ordinary course of business e.g. loans and repayments (above £25m); foreign currency transactions (above £25m).
4. Major investments or disposals above £30m or if the monetary sum is less than £30m the acquisition or disposal of interests of more than 2 per cent in the voting shares of any publicly quoted company or the making of any take-over bid for any publicly quoted company of whatsoever value.
5. Risk management strategy.
6. Treasury policies (including foreign exchange exposures).

Miscellaneous

1. Changes in the Trustees or rules of the Company Pension Scheme.
2. Changes in the rules of employee share schemes and the allocation and grant of employee share options.
3. Political donations.
4. Prosecution, defence or settlement of litigation (involving sums above £1m or being otherwise material to the interests of the Company).
5. Internal control arrangements.
6. Health and safety policy.
7. Environmental policy.
8. Directors' and Officers' liability insurance.
9. Directors' interest in shares and share options.
10. Directors' external interests.
11. Use of common seal.

It was further suggested and AGREED that this matter be reviewed in twelve months' time.

Figure 2.1   A FTSE 50 company

Role of the board

The Parent Company is ultimately responsible for policy. It has to ensure that the Group's public and legal obligations are met and within this broad generality it delegates responsibility for executive action to individuals, Committees and Board as appropriate. In practice the Parent Board will retain exclusive decision-making power in relation to capital expenditure and disposals exceeding £2m in value, senior appointments at the level of Divisional Chief Executive and above and Officers of the Company. The Board will also review all financial information which it requires to enable it to determine dividend policy, the capital structure of the company and any financial matters having third party relevance.

The Board shall retain authority in respect of any proposed changes in the Company's statutes.

Figure 2.2   A FTSE 100 company

Committees of the board

Role

In order to ensure greater depth of understanding, committees of the board are an effective way to raise standards, provide the required level of reassurance and obtain greater coverage by directors. The most important committees are the audit, the remuneration and the nominations committee.

The audit committee

Cadbury is quite clear about an audit committee's importance, how it should be constituted and what the agenda should be. Key points are:

- They should be formally constituted as a committee of the main board to whom they answer and they should meet regularly, but at least twice a year.
- There should be a minimum of three members, all of whom should be non-executive and independent of the company.

- The external auditor, as well as the internal auditor (where that function exists) should normally attend along with other board members who would usually include the finance director and chief executive.
- The audit committee should have a discussion with the auditors without the executive board members present.

This Committee of the Board is one of the most important recommendations of Cadbury. We believe that it has the potential to materially improve corporate governance and, of course, add value to the company. The crucial fact is that it is independent, providing checks against the executive, with the ability to review systems and internal control, and where necessary requiring improvements. It is in a good position to review objectively the progress made where improvements to controls or systems have been agreed. The central piece of recurring work is to review fully the interim and final accounts. This, together with the detailed review with the auditors of the significant items raised for discussion, ensures that the board is fully informed of the quality of financial reporting and any major areas of disagreement with the auditors. This is an increasing responsibility of the board, as we will see later, for the whole question of internal control is currently being debated with the probability that directors will need to publicly report on this.

Finally, the audit committee has a role, if required, to decide impartially over any disputes between the management and the external auditor should this situation arise. This 'Court of Arbitration' is an important way to reinforce the independence of the auditors.

Critics of audit committee

Critics of audit committees argue that in many cases they are ineffective, are unnecessary where good controls are in place, and become preoccupied with meeting imposed requirements to the detriment of effectiveness. There is, we regret to say, some truth in these concerns. What are the reasons for this? First, many members of audit committees have not been properly prepared for this role. It requires time and training to build up a knowledge base of the principles of accounting or of accounting standards. Most non-executive directors have time constraints and very few have been offered any formal training. While their knowledge base will improve over time, we believe that regular, probably annual, training sessions are needed.

Second, the success of the audit committee will depend to a large extent on its chairman who chooses the agenda and keeps the meeting constructive as it moves towards the conclusion. A high level of interpersonal skills is needed to organise, control, elicit diverse views and constructively deal with conflicts. These qualities are not universally found at present.

Third, the informed chairman should build up relationships directly with the audit partner, with the internal auditor and the finance director. In practice, this investment of time is not always made, which often leads to the reduced effectiveness of the committee.

Fourth, we expect a great deal of our committee members, and the task can be onerous at times and certainly time-consuming. Payments made for the extra work and responsibility of chairing an audit committee are usually nominal or non-existent, which will have at least some implications for the time that is committed.

Although not strictly a matter solely for the audit committee, there is some public concern over audit firms continuing to audit a company's accounts over a long period. There are three distinct issues surrounding audit firms and their partners and how they interface with the company.

1. Should the audit firm be compulsorily rotated at the end of a specified period?
2. Should the audit partner be rotated? Currently, best practice is that the partner in charge of an audit must be changed each seven-year period.
3. Should the audit firm be allowed to do other work for the client?

Our own view is that the professionalism, integrity and objectivity of auditors is not compromised under the existing arrangements where partners are rotated each seven years and firms can undertake other professional work. We think that rotation of partners probably in a shorter time frame of three to five years is helpful and that there is nothing wrong with an accountancy firm providing audit and other services from another part of the firm. After all, they know the company, have a shorter learning curve and are trusted by the management.

The audit committee will have established that the audit fee is appropriate and that the auditors' work plan is adequate to give them the assurances required. They will also need to be able to judge if the whole of the arrangements are appropriate and that the auditors remain independent of the management.

The remuneration committee

Differing expectations

People with different perspectives will have different expectations of the remuneration committee. On the one hand there is a section of the community who believe that the main job of committee members is to keep the lid on executive remuneration. For example, there are trade unionists and other politicians who believe that the criterion to be used in fixing salaries is to limit top pay perhaps to a factor of the average workforce pay and with increases to be limited to the average negotiation with the workforce. There may be some attraction in reminding those agreeing pay policy that all levels in a company watch what happens at the top level. However, this approach is not necessarily in the company's – and therefore the employees' – best interest. Industries with low labour rates for the workforce, reflecting a high proportion of labour content, or relatively unskilled labour would not be able to attract the best managers to them. Instead, they would be seduced to high-tech or low labour areas where potential remuneration would be higher.

On the other hand, institutions have made it plain that remuneration policy must be more closely aligned with the interests of shareholders. Incentive schemes should be pitched towards those measures most closely associated with their interests and with trigger points based on challenging but achievable comparative targets. Increasingly, payouts will depend upon out-performance of an agreed peer group or, if this is genuinely difficult to specify, then out-performance compared with an index of total shareholder return. Almost all directors we spoke to agree these principles and recognise that their company's remuneration policy must be set in the broad environment which prohibits unjustified increases or excessive total remuneration. The debate, of course, centres around reasonableness! These directors understand the trend to put a cap on total top income, although some also note with irony there is also a cynical observation that a number of institutions show a degree of duplicity in pressing companies to limit or reduce remuneration of top people when their own organisation's pay is perhaps unjustifiably high.

Transparency

The whole area of executive director's pay is one where trust needs to be restored. Good governance has a major role to play, largely exercised through the remuneration committee which needs to be seen to be independent and professional. This is an area that will always excite a lot of interest given the different interest groups in a community. Therefore, transparency is required through full disclosure and with concise explanations that describe what is behind movements.

Since the Cadbury Report, a lot has already been done to improve the information given in the annual reports, especially of those companies who take good governance seriously. Perhaps the most challenging area on which to give good, clear information is in performance bonuses for executive directors. These can be either annual or longer term (three to five year) schemes. The challenge is to describe accurately how they are calculated, how the targets are challenging and in the best interests of shareholders but without writing a book! Non-executive directors are almost universally remunerated with fixed fees. This approach is totally appropriate provided that the fees are set at a realistic level which has regard for the time required and responsibilities that directors have. Those who chair the audit or remuneration committees should have higher fees and those who are members of those committees should receive more than directors who do not serve on them.

Performance bonuses

There are also divergent views on what is the best base for performance bonuses. Those most commonly used are:

1. Operating profit or pre tax profits. This may be related to the year-on-year increase (for example Sainsbury who pay a maximum bonus of 25 per cent if profits increase by 20 per cent). Alternatively, it can be in relation to achievement of targets or a fixed percentage of an increase in profits over a base level. For example, Rexam's scheme pays out 1.75 per cent of salary for each 1 per cent increase in group operating profit.
2. Earnings per share. While historically this measure was more widely applied, recent changes in accounting standards mean that this is not always an indication of year-by-year progress. To some extent, the IIMR (Institute of Investment Management Research) tries to normalise earnings by excluding unusual transactions such as exceptional charges or credits.
3. Cash flow. Again, this can be taken as performance against targets or annual year-on-year progress. Courtaulds Textiles is an example of a

company that has successfully used this measure to motivate their
executive team to put cash generation at the top of their agenda.
4. Total shareholder return. This includes both dividends and capital
    appreciation over the time being measured and may include a
    provision of performance relative to a peer group. This is more usual
    in the long-term schemes. Safeway Plc use this approach and their
    comparison group is amongst defined retailers.
5. Economic value added. This measure charges a business with its
    weighted average cost of capital on the total assets used each year in
    the business. Any surplus over this is used as the base for bonus.

There are supporters of each of these alternatives. The arguments are
around simplicity of understanding, measures that best reflect long-term
shareholder interest and how accurate or manipulable the measure is. For
example, economic value added is, in our view, the best measure to reflect
long-term shareholder value because all funds used are charged with the
imputed cost of debt and equity of the company. Unfortunately, it is not
so easy to understand or explain to all concerned.

Ernst & Young, in their July 1995 publication *Corporate Governance:
Remuneration Disclosures*, have come to their own conclusion based on
their survey. They believe it preferable to base performance targets on
shareholder return rather than accounting measures such as earnings per
share. The main reason given for this choice is that 'accounting measures
are inherently more judgemental and open to short term fluctuation than
market measures. There is at least circumstantial evidence that decisions
as to accounting treatment of some items may be being influenced by the
impact on bonus payments.'

This, if true, is a serious situation for it means that the accounts cannot
be relied upon because they are manipulated and the auditor signs off on
this basis! We cannot accept that this is true. Further, to argue that it is
therefore better to go to the greater sanctity of the market price of shares
to pay bonuses because this is purer, is mistaken. Share prices can be
more readily manipulated than accounting measures. There is much more
evidence of a company management talking share prices up or down
based on their view of the outlook. Market makers make their profit (and
bonuses) based on movement in share prices. Putting these arguments
aside there are companies, of which Coats Viyella is one, in which there is
higher volatility of share price because of the industry; in other cases the
same effect on share price can be achieved by trading a relatively small
number of shares.

The choice of the best measure is one of the judgements a remuneration committee will make. It must be well informed of the alternatives and understand which of these is most closely aligned with the needs of the business and hence the shareholders.

Overall objective

The most important role of the remuneration committee is to have an appropriate reward policy that can attract, retain and motivate directors to achieve the long-term goals of the company. Many companies operate in a worldwide theatre and reward policies must keep this in mind. Committee members will, of course, need to be sensitive to wider community concerns. It is therefore highly important that:

- The committee is, and is seen to be, independent with access to its own external advice.
- It has a clear policy on remuneration that is well understood and has the support of shareholders.
- Performance packages are aligned with long-term shareholder interests and have challenging targets.
- Reporting is clear, concise and gives the reader of the annual report a bird's eye view of policy payments and the rationale behind them.

The nominations committee

This ad hoc committee, usually chaired by the company chairman, is the vehicle by which new non-executive directors are brought for selection. Usually, they will discuss and agree the brief, choose the search firm, agree the shortlist and interview final candidates. Objectivity and independence is preserved using this approach. It is a fact that in the past appointments were made more from within the circle of the chairman to offer him or her support, especially if times turned difficult. With a few limited exceptions, this patronage is gone. However, as we observed in the opening chapter, this does not mean that there is wide approval of the composition of boards or of the quality of non-executive directors. Many institutions would like to have a real say before non-executives are appointed rather than rubber-stamping a new appointment at the next annual general meeting. They are strong in their views that there should be restrictions on the number of non-executive appointments that a director can hold and that cross-board appointments should be abandoned.

There is also a clear external view that non-executives do not meet the expectations held of them. While this is in part due to unrealistic expectations, others hold the view that they are nothing more than 'decorations on the Christmas tree'. The evidence we have is different. Most directors, we believe, take their role seriously, act professionally and do their best to give value. In most cases they receive inadequate preparation for the new role and insufficient induction to the specific company. These are value creation areas for the nominations committee to pursue, preferably through the chairman who needs to be motivated to this end.

Increasingly, non-executive directors will need to spend more time on their directors' duties if they are to do them well. Companies need to be sure that they reward accordingly and an appropriate level of fees will certainly be supported by the institutions. Consideration should especially be given to the significant extra work in chairing the major committees of audit and remuneration as well as the responsibilities that are attached.

The board and strategy

When we look back on the corporate failures scattered through history there are, in our view, some common themes. These include:

- A lack of checks and balances in the system, enabling unfettered power to remain unfettered.
- Inadequate financial controls and supervision from board level.
- Inappropriate, or, in some cases, no strategic direction allowing management to pursue random interests or at least to pursue opportunistic thrusts that are not strategically well founded.
- Management that is not up to the standards required in the modern business world.

The board need to be aware of each of these areas. However, in this section, we would like to dwell on the board's ability to overlook the strategic process and also to ensure that an appropriate management development and succession plan is in place.

Spending sufficient time on reviewing succession plans and the annual management development evaluation is an important role for the board. Top-level succession planning both for emergency cover as well as for a longer time horizon, say five years, is a most important part of a board's monitoring role. Succession planning is a required risk-analysis exercise of vital importance to the company and the results will show the depth of management being developed. The fact that real competitive advantage is delivered through the human resource is a convincing reason why the board should annually review management's development plans. It is our observation that this potentially valuable exercise is not universally included on all board agendas. This is an annual agenda item of at least equal importance as the strategic plan and is, in fact, an interrelated part of it.

The company board will wish to add value to the strategy process as directors are aware that this is a fundamental business process that sets the scene for future decisions on resource allocation. Each board of directors will need to decide specifically the most appropriate way for them to address the process. Some companies are relatively simple to understand with a single product group, limited competition, similar customers and restricted geography. However, this is probably the exception rather than the rule. Most non-executive directors need to find a way to obtain sufficient background information to make informed judgements. This requires an investment of time, often including separate information-gathering from visits to main sites and discussions with managers who do not normally attend the board meetings. It also argues against short-term appointments of non-executive directors of, say, three years as it is often only towards the end of that time that we see sufficient knowledge accumulation.

On strategy, companies approach their boards in different ways. Historically, management would prepare a background paper that would summarise the operating climate and then spell out the key strategic steps, indicating a likely financial outturn over the term of the plan. A presentation would then be given to the board by the executive. The board would question the executives, approve the plan, perhaps with a few reservations, and move to the next item on the agenda. While this was largely a 'rubber stamp' approach, the non-executive directors would use their skill and experience to pose questions that required thoughtful responses. It was an uneven 'contest' as the knowledge base was almost entirely in executive hands.

Increasingly, the board of directors is recognising that much more information is needed on strategy and much more time devoted to the appraisal of proposals put forward. Usually, this requires a separate, focused meeting on strategy alone. Adequate preparation is needed for this meeting including background information which at a minimum should include:

1. A market review to show the dynamics, competition and customer base.
2. An environmental scan to show those trends that are likely to have a significant impact on the industry and the particular company.
3. An objective analysis of past results to see if the strategy in place is working as expected. This will involve both financial and non-financial parameters and, where appropriate, will compare the company with its competition.
4. A statement of the proposed strategy and a summary of the financial outturn and key milestones as the strategy is implemented.

Timing of strategy review

Non-executive directors understand that this is a key area where they need to be better informed and to improve their contribution. If the strategic agenda is not properly addressed, it can result in an under-optimisation of shareholder value or, in the extreme, a serious decline in net worth or even the collapse of the enterprise. Too often, the strategic process is not fully interrogated annually as the company continues 'to make satisfactory progress'. This is a mistake. Strategy review is just too important to be left to times when board intervention is essential. The board is almost compelled to address strategy when:

- A predator has made it clear that the company is undervalued and bids or is sitting in the wings about to bid (see Chapter 5).
- There is an unacceptable decline in earnings or a loss of confidence by the shareholder base reflected in a non-cyclical share price reduction.
- A new chief executive is about to be appointed, as change will almost inevitably follow and the board will want to influence this.

Each of these occasions emphasises the importance of strategy but the reality is that by the time at least the first two of these situations arise, it is too late for the board to make an effective strategic contribution. A company under threat from a predator or feeling disquiet amongst the shareholder base is not best placed to take the time to review strategic direction. The options with which it is likely to be faced will be more restricted and short term in focus.

Non-executive contribution

In our discussions with non-executive directors, we observed some important points. First, they are aware of the importance of strategy and they wish to improve their contribution to the process. Time is the great enemy for most as boards often run out of time when strategy is being discussed and non-executive directors do not have unlimited time to prepare for the debate. Second, the value of the strategic review is very dependent upon the willingness of the executive to be prepared to expose genuine areas of concern or difference of view for debate. Third, the conduct of the meeting and the role of the chairman can make the meeting of greater value. As one director said, 'Unless we can stop the executive from using almost all the allotted agenda time with their excellent presentations, we will not improve the process. We need to have 50 per cent of the time for debate.'

The approach taken by non-executive directors to the planning process is variable. There remain a few who do not always get time to read the pre-meeting documentation and comment 'off the cuff' at the meetings. Fortunately, these cases are becoming less and less. One of the most balanced responses to the question 'How do you, as a non-executive director, add value to strategy discussion?' was given by a senior figure who recently retired as a chief executive and is now on three boards. He said, 'I need to prepare well and that takes place throughout the year as well as reading the specific supporting information for the strategy review. I try to remember that my perspective must be one that directly reflects the shareholder and I must always be looking for the way to deliver the best long term value to them. My check list is simple, perhaps too simple. It is a six point check list as follows:

1. What simply is the current strategy and is it working?
2. What are the key drivers to achieve long-term advantage?
3. What are the significant changes driven by external circumstances including the marketplace that have implications for the business?
4. What resource and skills are needed? Does the company have them?
5. What results do the shareholders need and does the strategy deliver them?
6. Is there a resultant need to change the core work or processes of the company?'

This approach can be contrasted with the soul-searching of a non-executive director, Brian Ball, outlined in Case Study 2.1 which shows how the board failed to respond positively to danger signals that, with the benefit of hindsight, were clearly visible.

The successful chairman is fully aware that strategy is not just a once-a-year phenomenon. It is living in the company continuously. Therefore, throughout the year there will also be agenda items that have strategic implications or add to the board's overall understanding of the strategy. This is especially valuable when any short presentation is made by senior executives who are not normally seen at the board. This, too, enables the whole board to have a deeper understanding of strategy.

The strategic audit

There is a growing body of opinion, perhaps led in the United States of America, that argues that strategy is so important that it needs a formal review process. Many of the arguments for such a review are similar to some mentioned above. There is growing agreement on the importance of a special focus on strategy, taking whatever total time is needed to understand and evaluate it thoroughly. In addition, there is broad recognition that simply providing a slot on a regular board meeting is not adequate. As Gordon Donaldson, in his article, 'A New Tool for Boards: The Strategic Audit', in the July–August 1995 edition of *Harvard Business Review*, says, 'the typical board meeting is an inappropriate forum for raising serious concerns about a company's strategic direction. All who have served as board members know that attending a board meeting is rather like entering the on-ramp of an expressway at rush hour. You spend half the time getting up to speed and the other half trying to insert yourself into the bumper-to-bumper traffic, only to find that it is time to exit and try again a month later.' There must be many who would share that view!

The solution, according to Donaldson, is to appoint a sub-committee of the board with special oversight to audit the strategy in much the same way as an audit committee or remuneration committee is formed. This approach, it is claimed, allows for a continuing constructive dialogue between the executive and the strategic audit committee that should consist of non-executive directors. They would, amongst other things, agree what needs to be measured and ensure that the board is reviewing more relevant information throughout the year.

Genesis Plc

Genesis Plc is a fictitious name but the facts were provided from an actual case in the follow-up to our research where the non-executives were discomforted but did not take decisive action. The auditors were concerned that the accounts were becoming increasingly stretched each year as a result of management's drive to show year-on-year increases. Senior management below the chief executive level were increasingly worried about the strain on the last month of each half year to achieve respectable numbers and worried that they would not be able to 'find a rabbit to pull from the hat' in the following year. The events took place prior to the Cadbury Report and Genesis did not have an audit committee or a nominations committee. It did, however, have a remuneration committee which the executive chairman felt was helpful to deflect any City criticism of the quite high salaries paid to him and the top few executive directors.

However, let us start at the beginning and see this company through the eyes of one of the non-executive directors whom we will call Brian Ball. This was his first appointment as non-executive director and he was excited by the prospect when telephoned by a head hunter who had been retained to carry out the search. During the discussion with the head hunter Brian was flattered that there was strong reference to his marketing and business skills being very relevant and that there would be only two names going forward to the chairman. The head hunter described the chairman as a very strong personality who had risen through the company ranks and was chairman and chief executive. He advised Brian that the chairman was concerned to pick a visionary, not a penny-pincher. His salary was high, he was money driven and would be turned off by a lack of understanding of the need for high rewards. This was not seen as a problem as Ball believed in paying well, based on objectively measured success.

The interview with the chairman went well. He was charming, gave every indication that he wanted quality non-executives. He talked freely about the other directors' strengths and weaknesses and a little about the fundamentals of the three international businesses that made up the group. Later, the company secretary sent out two years' annual reports, the minutes of the past two or three directors' meetings together with financial accounts for the year to date and a broad outline of the budget. The introductions to the board members were made at Brian's first directors meeting.

The process for appointing new non-executives was for the chairman to advise that he was going about this task, use a head hunter he trusted well and advise the directors about progress. Prior to an appointment the candidate's c.v. was circulated to see if any director had objections. No one on the board could recall there being objections to any proposal put forward for a non-executive director.

Brian's first two years with the company went quite well as it made satisfactory progress and the share rating positively responding to the confidence of the chairman/chief executive. The unusual characteristic was the heavy loading of sales in the final month of each half year. The company would have a nail-biting five months when it was usually behind plan and in month six the orders and profits would come in to bring the group almost back on track. In some half years 100 per cent of the profits were made in month six and in the much larger second half as much as 60 per cent of that half's profit depended upon the last month. This was possible as many Genesis products were sold through national distributors who on-sold direct to the product users.

Although the company was making profit progress in most years, cash flow was poor and gearing was high. This was not helped by the numerous, usually small opportunistic acquisitions that were made on the recommendation of the executive. Often the strategic value of these was not especially clear but the projected financial success was worthwhile as often the management saw good synergy benefits. The proceeds of one rights issue were taken up, largely as a result of many such acquisitions.

Following the Cadbury Report, an audit committee was set up under a non-executive director who was in reality the leader of the non-executives. In fact, there were only three non-executives from the total board of nine directors. One was a retired executive director who was close to the chairman. The audit committee evolved its agenda but spent most of its time reviewing the half-year and full-year accounts, accounting standards and the financial information in the annual report. They became increasingly discomforted over time at the loading of the wholesale trade every six months in order to make respectable numbers. The trade would

take discounts for this together with extended credit an
not buy anything much for the next three or four mo.
accounts were stretched some years with expenses amorti
two years, a change in depreciation policy, allocation of c
substantial extraordinary or exceptional provisions as w .. as
others. As one director commented, 'management manage to find
an unexpected benefit in the last month of every year's accounts'.

After three years of this, the auditors indicated that they were
unhappy with the stretching of accounts and trade loading. The
chairman and finance director were not pleased with the auditors'
comments and some friction resulted, although it was agreed to set
down accounting policies more clearly and to phase out over the
next 18 months the excessive trade loading. However, the audit
partner was changed as management felt that they could no longer
work with him, and justified the need for change on the grounds of
personal chemistry differences.

It was also clear that the company was entering into an even more
difficult year ahead and that analysts' expectations would need to
be reduced. During the previous year a new chief executive was
recruited after a proper search and proper due diligence. He was an
able businessman but not a strong enough character to take issue on
any major matter with the chairman. However, in his third year of
service it was clear to the board that he was not at all confident
about the expected outturn for the current year and that the
company was again in need of a rights issue. The board's response
was to batten down the hatches and cut all development
programmes and capital spend. The financial results were very
poor and the company was lucky to survive and retain its
independence. During this time total remuneration remained high
even though performance bonuses were more subdued than
management expected. Salary increases were paid annually and all
salary comparisons were based on an international scale as the
executives were seen to be internationally mobile. A new management team was appointed as fortuitously the chairman was due to
resign on age grounds and this date of retirement was marginally
advanced. The board has since been reshaped, as was the company,
by focusing more completely on a much narrower, more strategically justified business.

Brian Ball resigned just prior to the very bad results being
announced. He did so on the grounds that his time commitments

precluded him from being as involved with Genesis as he felt was necessary. His private discussions with the chairman about his real concerns were not well received and he judged he could not make progress. On reflection, Ball makes these observations:

1. The strategy was neither precise nor clear. Management were able to take opportunistic actions because it appeared to be in line with a vague strategy. There were no real priorities and insufficient focus.
2. The chairman in reality had no balance to his strong, deeply held views. Having a full time chairman and chief executive did not help give clarity to the executive decision-making process.
3. A culture of high reward led to inappropriate business behaviour by executives (trade loading for example) that destroyed business values.
4. The company accounts were stretched and insufficient attention paid to cash flow.
5. There were coded warnings from the auditors that were not picked up. The case for the resignation of the audit partner was not independently tested by the audit committee.

The question he cannot really answer is whether he should have taken a more public view on resigning, giving indications as to why he was not comfortable staying on.

Perhaps reflecting Professor Donaldson's financial background, the approach suggested also focuses on appropriate financial indicators, thereby devaluing the wider strategic and competitive insights. In our view, the question of strategy can be addressed productively by the whole board provided a satisfactory structure and sufficient time is found. We do not see the need to create another board committee which would be capable of providing further distinction between the executive and non-executive elements of the board. Indeed, we would be concerned about the effect of consigning 'strategy' to a sub-group of the board. Strategic direction-setting must be, and must be acknowledged to be, central to the board's purpose.

The 'ideal' board

Is there some ideal or model for the future that can be aspired to? We will make some concrete suggestions in Chapter 9, but for the moment we suggest that the principles summarised in Figure 2.3 should inform board structures and processes.

Composition and balance	• Chairman and chief executive split • Minimum of three non-executives • Compulsory audit, remuneration and nominations committees
Board's own governance	• Terms of reference • Items reserved for board • Formally appraise board's working • Sufficient number of board meetings • Occasional meetings of non-executive directors with the CEO
Board agenda	• Agenda covers key decision areas, strategic and management development items • Well documented, timely • Always sufficient, concise information • Sufficient time
Non-executives (NEDs)	• Independently selected to a formal brief • Initial three-year term with probable renewal of a further three years • Formal induction • Training updates • Required to own shares • Appropriately rewarded
Culture	• Sets the tone for the company • Openness • Shareholders' interests paramount
Commitment to communicate	• Review investor relations programme • Annual report a window on the company • Best practice in disclosure
Management synchronised	• Think and act like shareholders • Appropriate incentives • A significant shareholding • Properly monitored • Comprehensive succession plans

Figure 2.3 The 'ideal' board

To set the scene, the role of the board is made easier if it has the right shareholders! We will see in a later chapter how the ownership agenda impacts upon the company. American authors such as Monks and Minow observe the increasing trend, which they view as positive, of relationship investing which provides a long-term shareholder platform for the company. Warren Buffett is a case in point. This view is supported by Michael Porter who has observed in his research report to the Council on Competitiveness (p. 91) that 'Perhaps the most basic weakness of the American system is the transient ownership in which institutional agents are drawn to current earnings . . . . The long-term interests of companies would be better served by having a smaller number of long term or near permanent owners whose goals are better aligned with the corporations.' This argument is similar to the teenager who argues that life would be easier if one's parents were different! At least in the medium term, a company is not going to find life easier by choosing different shareholders!

Composition and balance

The Cadbury Report recommended the split of the two key roles of chairman and chief executive. Where, for special reasons, this was deemed inappropriate, a clear leader of the non-executives was to be appointed. Since this report, the case for the split in roles and for no exceptions is stronger. It is a clear element in providing appropriate and effective checks and balances. Current practice supports this view with available research showing almost full acceptance of this principle. As an example, Richard Bostock of Leeds Business School, in his September 1995 paper to the British Academy of Management's Conference, tabled his research showing that only five of his 100 companies researched do not split the roles or at least have a strong independent deputy chairman if the roles are combined.

In order to get the spread of experiences required to staff up the necessary committees, there should be at least three non-executive directors. This will also provide the resource to chair the audit and remuneration committee which, along with the nominations committee, should be an integral part of good governance.

Board's own governance

To our surprise, there is not a great deal of formality about the board's own governance even though this is a key item for the chairman of the board. Many companies since Cadbury have reserved items for the board's oversight and decision but some of these agendas are vague. They are useful only for showing the auditors to allow them to sign off as complying with Cadbury. The spirit of Cadbury is more important.

In our experience, it is helpful to set down terms of reference for the board, including how it sees its main role and how it will govern itself. The board should then identify items reserved for its decision-making process. This will not only set the tone but will provide a benchmark for how the board will formally appraise its workings. This appraisal process is not something that the average chairman appears to be comfortable with. Often, the idea will be dismissed as unnecessary, for a thoughtful chairman will know instinctively if the board is operating well. Therefore, any request to review how the board works may well surprise the chairman and be taken as a criticism of his style. One non-executive director told us that after two years on a board he made some time to see the chairman to talk about his contribution which he felt could be improved with encouragement from the chair. He asked if the board agenda could be amended to have fewer informative presentations and more time on strategy.

This well-known United Kingdom chairman was surprised by the approach and more than a little defensive. He responded that if he felt that any non-executive was not performing or did not have a good attendance record he would 'have a quiet word in their ear'. On the question of the agenda, the chairman observed 'that the present format has been well appreciated over the years by the full board but he would take soundings'. Some minor changes were made to the agenda but the non-executive was at least mildly disappointed over the encounter.

We deal more fully with board evaluation in Chapter 3. The board, led by the chairman, must agree the way it operates and the number of occasions that it meets. Certainly, there is value, perhaps once or twice a year, to find an occasion for the non-executives to meet with the chief executive to discuss informally issues of interest. This is often helpfully achieved by a dinner, as the more relaxed atmosphere makes it plain that there is no formality about this meeting.

Board agenda

Each year the board should look at the balance on the agenda. There should be satisfaction that the regular agendas cover the key decision areas regularly required giving the right balance to strategic and operational issues and to financial and non-financial issues, especially those involving key people.

Given the crucial importance to the company's long-term performance, a separate meeting to focus on strategy, management development and succession plans should be provided in advance of the main meeting and during the meeting there should be plenty of time for discussion and debate.

In general, the board should determine the level of detail and scope of information required to support the agenda, giving three clear days to assimilate this prior to the meeting. Supplementing this, on a regular monthly basis, the board should decide what key data it needs to keep it informed between meetings. Some boards have a gap of eight to twelve weeks in the 'holiday season' and this is a good occasion for the chief executive to provide an update report to act as a bridge between meetings.

The agenda must always be thoughtfully prepared to provide the balance already referred to but, additionally, it must allow sufficient time for the key items to be properly aired and decided.

Non-executives

This is such an important area that it is the subject of a special chapter. However, in the context of the 'ideal board' it is helpful to make some brief observations here.

Firstly, the non-executive must owe his or her allegiance to the shareholders. Friends of the chairman or those with cross-directorships should exclude themselves. In order to avoid patronage from the chairman, the new directors should be independently chosen to a formal job specification using ProNED or one of the firms of search consultants. While the initial term should be three years, an extension of three years is desirable if mutually agreed by the individual and the chairman. Our research in the opening chapter showed that a number of institutions would like to be informed of proposed new appointees prior to their appointment and we believe this pressure is likely to increase over time.

Companies need to provide a formal induction programme which is likely to be a minimum of a couple of days of direct contact as well as making time to read appropriate background papers. This is an area where an uplift in standards is necessary. There is also no good reason why at least every two years non-executives should not undertake some top-up formal training. This needs to be encouraged by companies, the Institute of Directors and the stock exchanges around the world.

If non-executive directors are to represent shareholder interests we believe it is good practice for them, as with all directors, to own shares in the company within three months of appointment to the board. Finally, they need to be rewarded for the increased time and responsibility taken on board. It is likely that remuneration increases of around 50 per cent above today's level will be needed to get the right balance.

Culture

The board sets the tone and the standards for the company. Its actions must demonstrate the spirit of openness which is essential in good governance and in restoring trust within the wider community. It goes without saying that shareholders' interests are paramount.

Commitment to communicate

Openness requires a commitment to communicate to all interest groups. Here, we focus on shareholder communications. The board should, at least annually but perhaps twice a year, review its investor relations programmes. It should see the feedback from shareholders to ensure that management are addressing concerns and are communicating in a consistent, clear way.

The annual report and the report covering the interim results are a clear window on the company. Companies that follow best practice will use these reports as an opportunity to objectively review the progress against strategic and financial benchmarks. The reports will fully incorporate best practice in disclosures.

Management synchronised

Management must be fully in tune with the company's objectives and the value creation agenda to enhance long-term value to the shareholders. The challenge for the board is to allow management all the freedom they need to carry out this task yet to ensure that there is a satisfactory control mechanism to allow the board to exercise its responsibility for oversight of the company's actions. Clearly, at the outset the company must attract and retain the best talent and ensure that they are well prepared to drive up value for shareholders.

In addition, incentive packages need to be devised to ensure that management are rewarded in line with shareholder goals. This is likely to include a large element of performance-related pay weighted to the longer term and with the greater part paid out in deferred shares. We also believe there is a good case to be made for all executive directors to hold and retain a significant stake in the company. Over time, this could well approach the equivalent in shares of a year's income.

Finally, the board must satisfy itself that the management direction is compatible with objectives by ensuring that their efforts on management development and succession plans are synchronised. The best boards will ensure comprehensive plans in this area are in place and will make it their duty to know many of the key players at the top level in the business.

3 Evaluation – A Tool for Improved Corporate Governance

Introduction

In Chapter 2, we dealt with the role of the board, and, in our suggestions concerning the board's own governance, we urged that there should be a formal appraisal process to review the board's workings. Directors need to be satisfied that there are clear objectives and procedures for the board, and they need a process for measuring their own performance. That process of formally evaluating performance will receive greater prominence as boards of directors increasingly find themselves under public scrutiny.

Boards are having to adjust to these changing circumstances, in some instances having to change behaviours, whilst trying to ensure continued diligence. In the words of Gordon and Pound:

'Instead of episodic, confrontational challenges for control, CEOs and directors will find themselves subjected to continuous, ongoing scrutiny from both active investors and major long term institutional investors, who will seek to engage in substantive debate about specific corporate policies and overall corporate performance . . . . The new governance process is based on continuing dialogue and debate among key, long-term institutional and other investors about specific, substantive aspects of corporate policy.'

This public scrutiny and critical examination of boards has occurred mainly because of investors and other shareholders taking the view that some firms could be operating more effectively and that there can be reasons for failure that are, to some extent, preventable. Increasingly this perception is evidenced by legislation and regulation aimed at a clearer identification of directors' responsibilities, with the aim of better corporate governance. It is apparent that greater responsibility and expectations are falling on the shoulders of the board chair. Indeed it is not an exaggeration to assert that, in the new environment, there will be greater risk attached to holding directorships. Media reports state that companies' resources are being wasted due to failings in corporate governance duties. Yet, by and large, few people focus on board performance until there is a crisis; few directors and even fewer boards address the issue of performance evaluation. By contrast, most board members are already familiar with evaluation of their own efforts in other arenas, such as work, school or sports, and would not be likely to tolerate this type of performance neglect in the senior company staff whom they govern.

One of the mechanisms for prevention of poor company performance is for the board to be effective in executing its role and responsibilities. Improvement in performance can occur only if time is made available to take stock of what is happening. The board has the strength and authority to select, lead and direct management to the extent that it *is* the board and not the management which ultimately drives the success or failure of the company. It is the board which selects the CEO and monitors how the company performs in line with the objectives and strategy to which the board has agreed.

As investors become more educated about these performance relationships, and as governments become more sophisticated about the role of the board versus the tasks of management, it is likely that scrutiny of boards' actions will escalate. Therefore, it is vital that boards ensure they are acting as effectively and efficiently as possible. To facilitate this, it is necessary that boards have in place appropriate accountability mechanisms.

One such method is evaluation of board performance. This chapter will discuss what evaluation is, why it is important, and how to develop and implement such a system. There is no one correct way to do this, as consideration must be given to the individual firm, the dynamics of the individuals, the business environment, and so on. However, there are certain common planning features that can be adhered to, such as objectivity, inclusion of all affected parties, etc. (An assumption of this chapter is that there is no role duality with the chair and the CEO, which certainly accords with best practice.)

Evaluation: what is it?

Performance evaluation is a flexible, dynamic process that includes the act of setting goals and standards for performance. These goals need to be measurable and achievable. After this is completed, a system that allows regular evaluation of these criteria for each director and the board as a whole should be developed and implemented.

Evaluation should be used to identify how the board is currently performing, so that planning for the future can occur. The purpose of evaluation is not to be critical, or to act in a policing role, although this is sometimes the final outcome. Evaluation should be considered an integral part of the overall board planning process, and to be successful evaluation should be non-confrontational. The fact that evaluation is not seen regularly in current practice, since it is difficult to develop and implement, is not in itself sufficient reason for not attempting to phase it into board practice.

There is evidence to suggest that current board practice usually does not include any form of evaluation – whether it be of individual directors or the board as a whole. However, evaluation may occur on an ad hoc individual basis – for example, when a director is invited to join a board. The invitee often ascertains whether or not they believe the board is effective before they accept the invitation. Yet performance evaluation of any position, not just the board, helps ensure accountability and effectiveness of people in their roles. It is one way of helping to overcome group anonymity and elusive standards that have been seen in boards in the past.

In addition, evaluation is useful for engaging in a process that enables feedback to occur. Zander writes of a *feedback cycle*: 'A board that evaluates its performance and changes its objectives, methods, or both, is engaged in a *feedback cycle*.' He goes on to outline in diagrammatic form the feedback cycle in a governing board (see Figure 3.1).

Zander states that these are typical stages in feedback. The first three stages are self-explanatory, with stage four showing members observing any deviations between the original goal and the board's performance through the gathering of information. The fifth stage is one of comparing and reflecting: '[D]esires that members have for the board, their personal motives and pressures from external agents influence members' reaction to this evaluation. [In] the sixth [stage], if the deviation between the board's level of attainment is larger than is tolerable to members, the members take steps to reduce this discrepancy, either by changing the board's actions in the future or by changing the group's goal'. This links

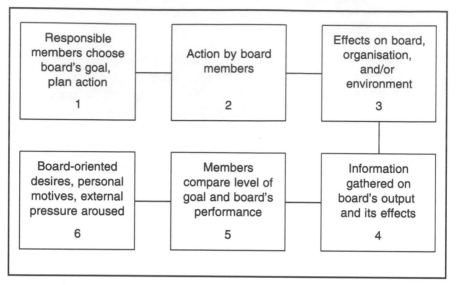

Figure 3.1   Feedback cycle in a governing board

Source: A. Zander, *Making Boards Effective*, Jossey-Bass, 1993.

back to, and includes, the first stage in box one of Figure 3.1, reflecting that feedback is an ongoing process.

Zander goes on to say that the feedback loop reveals the relationship between the board's performance and what is desired. This is how the feedback cycle links with board evaluation. For evaluation to be possible, there needs to be discussion and critique as to what is happening, why, and discussion on how it can be improved. This is feedback. In addition to understanding the feedback cycle, it is important to understand the elements of performance.

Demb and Neubauer state that evaluation of performance is done in terms of its outputs, inputs and the quality of the process that is used to produce both. Figure 3.2 also suggests that evaluation can relate to the type of output that it is relevant to measure. In addition, the figure points out that the aim of the board should be to add value to the company at the same time as gaining personal satisfaction, through the intrinsic value of being on a board and doing a job well. We can see that if the directors cannot give quality input, then the quality of the output will be greatly reduced. Various resources, such as technology, information, etc., enable a board to execute its role well. However, it must be noted that the board functions on a dynamic basis, and that this model does not reflect this.

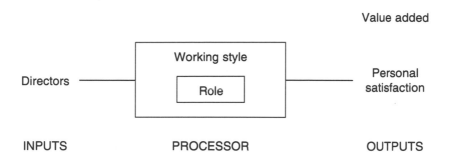

Figure 3.2   Elements of performance

SOURCE: A. Demb and F. F. Neubauer, *The Corporate Board: Confronting The Paradoxes*, Oxford University Press, 1992.

Implementing evaluation: the process, the pitfalls

How does a board get to the position of being able to set questions and tasks for itself, such as those in the following section? A process needs to be actioned that reflects the decision to change to a system where evaluation is the norm. As with any change management, there is no one right way to do this. However, some work needs to precede any change, and there are particular efforts that must be made during the change. Once changes have been made, in order to ensure continuation of the success brought by those changes, evaluation of the new system must occur as required.

If there has been no previous evaluation system, or even acknowledgement that evaluation of the effectiveness of the performance of the board is useful, then usually there are some fundamental changes that have to occur before planning of the objectives can begin. There must be a change in the philosophy, structure and culture of the board, so that there is consensus that evaluation is necessary and is possible in a manner that suits the board as a whole. As with any change management, there is a need to have a leader of the process who can take the initiative to continue, even when the going gets tough. As the chairman is the leader of the board, and has the authority to manage change in the board, it is vital that the chairman is driving the need for change; in essence, the chairman is the 'project champion'.

It is just as necessary that the *process* of developing the evaluation system is objective, as that the evaluation *itself* is objective. Although the board dynamic, according to which the chairman and directors are working as much as possible as a team, makes objective evaluation a difficulty, it is vital that such objectivity is striven for if the evaluation is to be of any benefit.

The actual sequence of events for implementation will depend on the individual company, the board and the drivers of the change process. Although the process cannot be divided into neat pieces and stages that follow a logical sequence, there are particular features that should be evident if success is to occur. These are as follows:

- *Vision*   The key driver, that is, the chairman, must have a clear vision as to what will be gained from implementing evaluation and how the board is going to get there. This vision must be articulated to all members of the board and they must understand the reasoning of the leader. It is at this stage that debate as to the advantages and disadvantages of the evaluation should occur.
- *Timing*   Consideration needs to be given to the issues and events that are current at the time of implementing evaluation. For example, it would not be easy to introduce evaluation if the chairman was already in significant disagreement with a director, for it could be seen as producing some form of policing and/or disciplinary mechanism. In such circumstances, evaluation probably would not produce the positive effects it can have, such as planning and increasing performance outcomes.
- *Planning*   The chairman must plan the process of change, including input from the rest of the board. The plan must be flexible so that any necessary amendments can be incorporated. The board should consider whether it wishes to employ external expertise, in the form of consultants, to help model and introduce evaluation procedures. The main advantage of using consultants is that they can be useful if there is a need to discuss sensitive matters. An outsider offers directors a neutral person with whom to discuss issues privately. The largest risk of using consultants is that they can become 'the chairman's person'. Collective board trust can then decline, or there can be a general reluctance to take responsibility for turning recommendations into action. To help prevent these negative outcomes, and to make the best use of a consultant, it needs to be decided who has responsibility for actioning the recommendations, who hires the consultant, who sets the scope for evaluation and who makes the decision as to when a consultant is required. For boards initiating evaluation for the first time, an outside consultant would be best to help formulate the

process, as the board will be busy enough with the detailed discussions without developing the process too.

The advantages of having a self-evaluation without the use of a consultant are that it can enhance the group's cohesiveness and give more ownership to the recommendations, making implementation more likely. Disadvantages include the fact that sensitive issues may be avoided, and that problems with the chairman's behaviour may not be investigated or addressed.

It is at the planning stage that the chairman should be trying to perceive and anticipate any implementation difficulties that may arise. Planning also involves the setting of objectives. These objectives stem from the agreed performance standards and provide for ease of performance measurement.

- *Organisational Design* It is necessary to ensure that the structure of the board, and perhaps even of the organisation, is conducive to accepting and responding to the proposed changes. It is futile to try to introduce evaluation into a structure that cannot support the process. The necessary structure will be entirely dependant on the form of the evaluation procedures to be introduced – that is, whether they are relatively formal or informal – and the current operations of the board.

- *Ownership* For any impending change, it is vital that the key affected players have ownership of the plan if sabotage is to be avoided. Ownership creates an environment where team effort and ongoing evaluation is effortless and productive. In relation to ownership, Ronald Nichol states that:

> 'Buy-in usually has two phases: logical and emotional. Typically people buy in logically when they have an opportunity to gather and discuss the facts and their implications. They do not buy in emotionally until they feel they own a plan for the change and know what is in it for them.'

- *Communication* A well-functioning board will have clear and effective internal and external communication at all times. This is especially vital in times of change. However, despite all efforts, communication may not work in the expected fashion, especially if the introduction of evaluation is going to challenge vested interests or compete with other priorities. In these circumstances, it is best to use continuous factual information as to the expected benefits the change will bring. Directors will thus be able to see that it is not a personal affront to be evaluated, but merely a function of planning and improving performance.

It is sensible to acknowledge that not all players will be able to accept and adapt at the same price to the introduction of evaluation. In fact, in some instances it may be that a particular individual will not be able to make the transition at all, and a plan of how best to manage this situation should be made early in the planning stage. It is ultimately the responsibility of the chairman to ensure that this occurs.

Conducting board performance evaluation

'The key is to create a process that allows board members to explicitly discuss board effectiveness and to implement whatever changes are deemed necessary.' (Demb and Neubauer)

As already mentioned, each board will vary according to personal dynamics, industry, size of organisation, etc. Although it is generally accepted that evaluation of boards and individual directors is useful, there is not widespread agreement about how the evaluation should be carried out. For many boards, the question of how to implement a process that allows for objective, fair and regular evaluation is too difficult to address at a functional level.

Criteria and questions need to be specified for evaluation of the board. This list will not be short, because it must include all factors that combine to create an environment where the board can make a real contribution. Before this, however, two questions must be answered: (a) who should do the evaluation?, and (b) when should it be done? Before evaluation can occur, the standards that the board wishes to be in place need to be identified. Demb and Neubauer set the criteria for evaluation in three categories: the directors, their role, and the board's working style. Their main points are summarised below:

The directors themselves

- *Intent, especially CEO/Chairman*: Chairman and CEO set context and lead board toward performance level. If they value the input of the board, they create a forum in which expertise and wisdom can be tapped

- *Selection, Nomination, and Departure*: Choose directors who will be loyal to company and stockholders. Brief on company performance during orientation. Handle departures carefully.
- *Composition and Balance*: Choose directors well – consider stature, integrity, courage, enthusiasm, experience and expertise. Ensure skill balance. No magic number as to size of board, but the precise number should reflect personalities involved.

The role: doing the right thing

Define a role – a set of functions and activities – that adds value.

- *Agreeing on a Board Mission*: Evaluation of the board's role asks the question: Is the board 'doing the right thing?' The development of a clear and shared understanding of its mission should be a primary goal for the board and top management of a company.
- *Defining the Portfolio:* Identify areas where the board can add value. How the board should allocate its time will differ from company to company. Ensure that by default agendas are not set by management.
- *Setting Priorities:* Priorities will depend on the company and its size. In the evaluation context, the board should consider whether it is giving the priorities the appropriate amount of time and attention.
- *The Board–Management Balance*: Address board–management power issue explicitly, to avoid power to management by default. Ask questions such as, Is the board proactive or reactive? Which decisions are delegated to management? Five types of involvement for the board – setting the vision, analysing options, implementing strategy, monitoring progress, and evaluating outcomes.
- *Legal Requirements:* These set minimum standards, but boards may choose to impose more rigorous standards upon themselves.
- *The Business Environment:* Conditions in the company's business environment should influence the board's involvement.
- *The Status of the Company*: Current stage of company development will reflect the level of board involvement required, e.g., expansion, retrenchment, etc.

The working style: doing things right

- *Size/Structure/Committees*: Committees focus on issues and help overcome the risk of ignorance.

- *Meeting Schedule*: Need to have enough meetings so that the board is not just performing a monitoring role. When evaluating a board, check this situation.
- *Information*: Is the board getting timely, correct information? Need more than operating figures to make strategic decisions. Need site visits to gain intuitive understandings.
- *Climate*: Climate must support constructive criticism. A few words describe climate features that are essential – frank, open, courteous, critical, interested, involved, direct and helpful.

Once all of these features are accepted as positive standards, then evaluation by measuring performance in relation to these, and possibly additional, standards can begin.

When evaluating, it is not just the board that needs to be considered. There are several elements in addition to the full board that require attention: individual directors, the chairman and the CEO. Examples of what is possible in each case follow.

The board as a whole

Together the board needs to discuss and review how far it has gone towards achieving its set objectives and missions, the overall board and company goals for the period specified. Evaluation of the board is the responsibility of the chairman and is carried out by the whole board. In an ideal situation, where the board is functioning using best corporate governance practices such as open discussion, consensus decision-making, etc., there may be no need for formal evaluation cycles. Efficiently functioning boards will review their practices and outcomes on an ongoing basis, making changes where necessary. This is an interactive and dynamic informal evaluation process.

Unfortunately, not many boards do function at this ideal level. For the majority, therefore, it is valuable for boards to have a more formalised system. This may include at least one meeting per year dedicated to discussing such issues as how the board feels about its level of functioning and its achievements. Informal networking, with individuals discussing how they feel things are going, is also useful.

Hugh Parker in his *Letters to a New Chairman*, goes a long way towards answering the operational question as to how practically to evaluate the board, stating that he has

'. . . not yet been able to define precisely a set of criteria for board performance that can be strictly applied to all boards. But I have developed a checklist of six questions that I believe can be used by a chairman to test the effectiveness of his own board – and from that, as a starting point, to decide what can be done to improve it

1:   Has the board recently devoted significant time and serious thought to the company's longer term objectives and to the strategic options open to it for achieving them? . . . have these been put in writing?

2:   Has the board consciously thought about and reached formal conclusions on what is sometimes referred to as its basic 'corporate philosophy' – i.e., its value system, its ethical and social responsibilities, its desired "image" and so forth? . . . codified or embodied in explicit statements of policy . . .

3:   Does the board periodically review the organisational structure of the company? . . . the senior appointments as a matter of course?

4:   Does the board routinely receive all the information it needs to ensure it is in effective control of the company and its management? Have there been any "unpleasant surprises" . . . that could be attributed to lack of timely or accurate information?

5:   Does the board require the managing director to present his annual plans and budgets for their review and approval? . . . monitor the performance of the managing director and his immediate subordinate managers in terms of actual results achieved against plans and budgets?

6:   When the board is required to take major decisions . . . does it have adequate time and knowledge . . . rather than finding itself overtaken by events, and in effect, obliged to rubber stamp decisions already taken or commitments already made?

Finally, there is one more question you might ask to test your board's effectiveness. If you accept the premise that it is for directors to direct and for managers to manage, what proportion of the board's time and attention *as a board* is devoted to the kinds of issues raised in the foregoing six questions, and how much to immediate issues of day-to-day *management?*'

Parker is obviously trying to focus the board on its role of governance through questions that create a sound base for role construction and evaluation. He leads the board to focus on the long-term vision that it should have, and the structure within which it and the organisation operate. He puts heavy emphasis on review of all that a board governs, including 'managing' the management to ensure that the board is getting adequate information to make well-informed decisions. Parker's list of six questions also helps a board focus on its responsibility to employ and oversee the quality of the CEO, as well as bringing in the critical issue of time. Having enough time to do the job justice is extremely important. Evaluation must look at how well how the board has managed its time, for, if poor time management is the norm, then the board will be more likely to make poor decisions and may even overlook some elements of its responsibility.

The board group appraisal can consider the obvious functions such as information flow and decision-making processes as well as the board's ability to raise and resolve issues, particularly difficult or emotive issues. One board's approach to this review is to identify a set of criteria that describe the quality of a meeting, or decision-making process. Each element is given end points, for example:

Confusing	⟷	Clarifying
Dominated	⟷	Participative
Passive	⟷	Active
Inefficient discussions	⟷	Efficient discussions, etc.

Questions are asked such as: Are the meetings confusing, or do they clarify issues? Are discussions dominated by one or two people, or do all participants get a chance to have input?, etc. The directors decide on their own personal rating of these elements on a scale of one to five, with the results being tabled for discussion. Rating against these and other elements then provides a focus for the board to discuss its effectiveness and thereby identify areas for improvement.

Individual directors

Depending on the composition of the board, evaluation of individual directors may need to be split into two streams: evaluation of non-executive and executive directors. In many countries, it is common for a sub-committee of the board to be set up to evaluate the executive directors. This sub-committee is often called the remuneration committee.

To have a sub-committee for this purpose, however, is not yet common practice.

All things being equal, evaluation of individual non-executive directors is the responsibility of the chair. Each chairman and board will have to decide which evaluation system works best for them. However, Demb and Neubauer state that:

'One of the most difficult tasks is the evaluation of individual director contribution. Evaluation of executives is usually a part of the board's overall assessment of company performance. However, assessing the performance of non-executives is difficult . . . Coming to grips with a non-performing outside member is an even more unappetising task for most boards.'

Discussions with individual directors should be held at least annually, but review of board, director and CEO performance should be ongoing, as stated above. The chairman should ascertain if individuals are happy with the way that the board is working and with other individuals' contributions to the board. Important points and contentious issues arising from these discussions should be brought to the full board for consideration and resolution. Evaluation without follow-up action to create change where it is required, is pointless.

The chairman should lead the development of a position description that envelops the areas described below. This should include active input from the directors at all times. The position description should embrace the standards that are expected and outline the programme that is in place to follow up on these standards. The position description must be quantitative where possible and should include the role of the board, criteria for competence/expectations, performance standards, outline of how directors will be rewarded and, if required, disciplined, as well as details of how evaluation will take place, its frequency and who will carry it out.

Evaluation of directors should be conducted by the chairman, seeking an emphasis on the director's contribution individually and to the group. Criteria should be set for evaluating director's competencies, covering such areas as:

- *Independence:*
  Confident, courageous, has a free-standing posture, avoids conflicts of interest, free thinker, etc.

- *Preparedness:*
  Briefs self thoroughly, spends extra time when necessary, knows key staff, respects confidentiality, knows organisation and the industry, understands statutory and fiduciary roles.
- *Practice as a Director:*
  Thoroughly prepared, does any necessary homework, avoids surprises, asks probing questions, insists on getting all necessary information, participates on committees as asked, active in furthering education of directors, participates constructively in meetings, etc.
- *Committee Activity:*
  On standing committees exhibits ideas, enthusiasm, uses ability and influence constructively, does homework, understands the process of committee work and relationship with management, etc.
- *Development of the Organisation:*
  Makes penetrating suggestions on innovations, strategic direction and planning, knowledgeable about trends and externalities, understands the impact of ownership on productivity, questions appropriately, helps win the support of outside organisations, investors, customers and suppliers, etc. (Mueller)

This process will then lead to an action plan for director development.

A task that should be given such consideration is *how* the evaluation might be performed. It may be that there is a mix of both formal and informal sections of the evaluation. Formal would constitute having a written agreed set of objectives that are set at a specific time each year (or more frequently). There are several steps, adapted from Mark Michaels's paper on CEO evaluation, that are useful to follow if there are individual meetings for evaluation. The meeting should be non-confrontational, objective and informal if the best use is to be made of time and discussions. Michaels sets out the following steps:

1: The chairman should establish an open, non-procedural spirit, where two way communication is emphasised. To avoid the 'policing' feeling and resulting attitudes, the emphasis of the meeting should be on planning.
2: Start by reviewing the tasks that had been set. It is important to start here, as tasks assessment is essentially objective, thus reducing the involvement of egos. By working on solutions to tasks that have been difficult or not quite completed, an atmosphere of problem solving will be create. This will help reduce any defensiveness on the part of the director.

3: Next move to discuss and evaluate behavioural issues, still focusing on the planning emphasis created in the initial stages of the meeting.
4: At the end of the meeting, the director and chairman should write up the individual objectives for the coming year.

Evaluating individual directors on an informal basis is often more comfortable for both the chairman and the director. This would take the form of a non-confrontational discussion. As suggested above, of course, the more ideally functioning board ensures ongoing, dynamic evaluation. Assessment will be against the standards that the individual director and chairman have already agreed at the beginning of the period, such as those previously listed. Once again, these objectives need to be tailored to the board's particular requirements and circumstances.

If a director is under-performing against the agreed criteria, then his/ her fate should be handled carefully. Unless it is a case of gross misconduct, the departure of this individual is not usually critical enough to warrant threatening the image and reputation of the company in the market and the business community. Boards that actually do attend to the problem of outside director non-performance use primarily two mechanisms to do so: a rule regarding retirement age and the creation of director terms, as well as individual meetings with the chairman.

The Chairman

The chairman is the heart of the board, the person with the ultimate responsibility for the organisation's governance. It is vital that the chairman is functioning efficiently in that role. It is difficult to identify common practice on this issue. One suggestion is for the chairman to stand down and put him/herself up for re-election at predetermined intervals. The intervals should have been decided upon by the full board, and could be annual or bi-annual. The board decides on evaluation criteria for the chairman, once again these being specific to the organisation. All objectives and criteria for chairman performance should be linked to the strategy of the company, company performance, board performance, and individual contribution.

A structure should be in place so that any dissatisfaction among the board regarding the chairman can be aired easily and addressed as an issue of importance. Two ways to attend to this are to set down a formal allocation of time to discuss the performance of the chairman; and/or, via informal discussion among the directors, arrange meetings and discussions outside the board room. Any issues arising should be taken to the next board meeting for discussion and resolution. To ensure this happens, a single director should be allocated the responsibility for making it an agenda item.

CEO evaluation

Almost invariably the CEO is a board member. Thus evaluation of this position requires addressing in this chapter. CEO evaluation is one of the more important duties undertaken by the board. The process should be positive, a part of the regular planning function and should provide the CEO and the board with a better understanding of how the organisation is performing in relation to the implementation of its strategies. Broadly, the evaluation should be carried out along the following guidelines:

1. *Establish task standards:*
   These are the outcome-based criteria.

   - Standards should be set through the CEO's work contract, the annual work plan and quantitative performance standards.
   - The contract should specify outcomes or actions for the CEO and progress against these should be assessed.
   - The work plan is the annual implementation plan for the company's strategies. As such, it is developed against a set of standards and quantifiable objectives.

   These objectives then form the criteria against which the CEO's performance can be evaluated. These may include financial ratios, human resource factors and, where possible, data from comparable companies.

2. *Establish functional standards:*
   This is a more difficult and subjective area of evaluation, since it involves *how* the CEO should perform. Areas of importance may be communication skills, financial management, etc. These behavioural criteria should be identified by each board on an organisation-specific

basis so that value can be added to the CEO through the evaluation process. The board should:

- Identify five to ten criteria that it considers essential to the performance of the CEO's role.
- Define these criteria as they relate to the organisation. These definitions must be clear and specific.
- Define the optimum performance level and the range of possible performance levels of the CEO, to measure against the set standards.

3. *Conduct the evaluation:*

   The board should meet without the CEO to discuss and reach agreement on its assessment of the CEO against the quantitative criteria mentioned above. The full board, excluding other executive directors, should then participate in the evaluation meeting with the CEO. This meeting should be as open, and have as much two-way discussion, as possible. Review of task evaluations should be completed first, as this area is less likely to be emotive and sensitive. The focus should be positive and should be on what needs to be done and how that can be achieved rather than accusations as to why something was not done. Behavioural issues should then be discussed. Again, the focus should be on planning, as opposed to attaching blame.

Summary

There is no denying that performance evaluation is a difficult process to install into board practice. Nor is it easy to establish and maintain its objectivity and effectiveness. However, it is vital to the long-term successful performance of a board of directors – especially in today's business climate, characterised by increasingly rapid change and ever closer scrutiny.

Evaluation is useful as it takes previously established standards, and measures outcomes against these standards. Evaluation helps prevent group anonymity and is useful for ensuring a feedback cycle that aids continuous improvement of performance. With the increasing responsibilities and accountability being placed on the board, in particular the chairman, performance evaluation may be an essential protective tool for the board of the future.

Appendix 1: A director's boardworthiness check-up

[From R. K. Mueller, 'A Director's Performance Appraisal', *Directors and Boards* (Spring 1993)]

Under these examination guidelines, the rating of *Honours* signifies director service of distinction with overall high effectiveness. *Pass* implies that the director is satisfactory on essentially all counts. *Fail* means that the director is unacceptably deficient in contributions, performance, or effectiveness.

The do-it-yourself check-up is a suggested thought process. It is not meant to be constraining or overly quantitative. Judgement as to which attributes are essential in order for a director to be effective will vary. This depends on the philosophy, concept, and policies of the board; the value systems of individuals on the board; the nature of the corporate enterprise; and the environment in which the corporation operates.

No two enterprises or boards are alike and, therefore, I can see no way to standardise these categories. This framework is offered only to start you thinking about the importance of personal effectiveness in the boardroom (Robert K. Mueller).

Competence as a director

Honours: Fits in well and with distinction. Personally competent. Effective presence. Experience. Influential. Respected. Outstanding peer relationships in profession, business, or community, and with other board members.

Rounds out board strengths, abilities, experience and subjective judgement.

Good communicator.

Ideologically oriented toward socio-economic philosophy relevant to corporate welfare and conduct and supports them.

Understands the difference between governing and managing a corporate enterprise.

Is clear on the long-term economic mission of the enterprise and the delicate balance with social accountability.

Pass: Meets most criteria above but may not be optimal when compared with talent available elsewhere.

Fail: Talents largely duplicative of others, or less rounded out. While similar talents are often useful, director is substantially below level of competence and experience of others. Absence incurs no handicap to board functions. Realistically, must be discounted as having significant input to soundness of decisions or effectiveness of board. Does not fit needs of corporation.

Independence

Honours: Thinks, speaks and acts independently, with confidence and courage.

Focuses on free-standing posture where independent decision is important.

Avoids real or apparent conflicts of interest.

Resists tendency of board toward a self-perpetuating protectorate unresponsive to change.

Is a free thinker.

Espouses a reasoned, independent directorate.

Does not behave independently for sake of being an iconoclast or a revolutionary character. Is objective when considering trade-offs and consequences.

Is also willing to risk rapport and collateral with chairman, board members, and chief executive officer in taking a reasoned, independent position.

Understands and supports proper, albeit complex, relationships of the board members with the chairman, the CEO and executive management.

Would relinquish directorship rather than be considered captive.

Pass: Respected for independent role

Not as prickly an independent as qualifications above.

Speaks up on critical matters requiring objective opinion.

Not captive of the chairman, chief executive officer, or other member of the board, although may be influenced at time by their dispositions toward matters.

Potential conflict areas – real or perceivable – are openly explored and an objective position is adopted.

Fail: Is a captive to members of board or outside parties.

Functions as surrogate for other interest.

Is primarily dependent on political currents.

Lacks will or courage to speak and act independently.

Preparedness as a director

Honours: Briefs self thoroughly. Shows sincere interest.

Spends extra time with chairman and CEO on relevant issues.

Knows key officers and some back-up managers.

Visits facilities as appropriate.

Exchanges views with others in corporate world.

Respects confidentiality.

Knows corporation's history, philosophy, style and strategic plans.

Keeps abreast of professional and international trends.

Preparedness as a director

Honours (cont.):	Understands statutory and fiduciary roles.
	Stays current on legislative and regulatory matters.
	Is a continuing student of corporate enterprise, governance and management.
	Exercises responsibility to shape policy and ensure continuing management.
	Keeps out of executive-administrative zone.
	Assists in corporate growth.
	Understands director and officer liability insurance protection and indemnification measures taken by the corporation for his or her personal protection.
Pass:	Is generally familiar with corporation's philosophy, opportunities and problems. Needs limited self-education on the business and director function.
	Is reasonably current with company and industry problems.
	Understands power separation between directorate and executive management.
Fail:	Little knowledge of, but some interest in, general state of company and industry.
	Sporadic self-briefing.
	Doesn't try very hard beyond attending meetings.
	Contributes little thoughtful input.
	Gets more from association than offers – in wisdom, reputation, advice, enthusiasm and support.

Practice as a director

Honours:	Thoroughly prepared.
	Does homework and understands reports and background materials.
	Communicates privately and constructively with chairman or chief executive between meetings.
	Avoids surprises.
	Asks probing questions focused on policy and strategy rather than tactics and details.
	Does not interrogate to show off knowledge.
	Director work is mostly talk and thinking.
	It is more symbol-intensive than labour-intensive.
	Insists on and gets information necessary for decision-making.
	Does not invade province of executive management.
	Conducts himself or herself so that corporation is satisfied with director's effectiveness.

Fulfils statutory and fiduciary requirements.

Keen ability to evaluate CEO, senior management and company performance.

Participates on committees when asked.

Key resource to management and board.

Introduces new thinking.

Active in civic affairs and furthering education of directors.

Pass: Generally prepared on issues.

Fulfils statutory and fiduciary role.

Reasonably able in evaluative role.

Participates intelligently and constructively at meetings.

Exhibits prior thought, interest and consideration rather than performs for peers' benefit, or to show that he or she is an interested director worth the fees.

Fail: Little evidence of study prior to meetings.

Use meeting time to develop background by asking questions dealt with in briefing papers.

Causes some frustration because of amateur performance.

Allows leadership to fall to others.

Misses meetings too frequently without legitimate excuse.

Discussion, if any, is often negative and unhelpful.

Really is not with it.

Cannot truly be considered committed, responsible or interested.

Committee activity

Honours: Serves usefully on at least one important committee.

Has ideas and enthusiasm.

Uses abilities and influence constructively.

Does homework.

Understands process of committee work, particularly relations with executive management.

Pass: Nominally loyal to committee responsibilities.

Attends meetings and carries out some duties with acceptable interest. Is definitely subordinate to the committee chairman.

Does little work on his or her own.

Relies on committee staff work.

Fair attendance.

Little effort exerted outside of meetings.

Committee activity (cont.)

Fail: Not particularly well-prepared and misses sessions frequently.

Uses committee time to think about assignment.

Brings no new thinking.

Often opposed to consensus without credible rationale.

Little sense of responsibility toward committee, even avoids assignments.

Operates passively without participative actions except for attending some scheduled meetings.

Development process of the corporate enterprise

Honours: Owns (but does not trade in) responsible amount of corporate stock in relation to own resources.

Makes penetrating suggestions on innovations, strategic directions and planning.

Knowledgeable about trends and externalities.

Understands the impact of ownership on productivity in a closely held corporation.

Recognises share owners as the only voluntary constituency whose relation with the corporation often does not come up for periodic renewal. Consequently, sees that in the development process, governance mechanisms protect shareholder interests and enhances shareholder value.

Questions officers in appropriate manner and at proper times on financial strategy.

Helps win support of outside organisations, customers, suppliers and investors.

Relates corporation to new business opportunities ethically through direct and indirect participation.

Positive force and independent thinker with interest in future directions and equity patterns of the corporation. Believes in conscious promotion of economic growth with social fairness.

Pass: Holds nominal amount of company stock.

Occasionally explores business issues with financial, commercial or technical community on behalf of company when encouraged to do so.

Average interest in conventional growth prospects.

Not particularly identified as a strong supporter of forward innovative programs, but does not unduly resist them.

Fail: Does not participate, even nominally, in furthering financial, commercial, or technical connections with the organisation, profession or industry.

If required by law, holds token amount of shares, but purchase is not usually of own volition.

Brings nothing substantive to deliberations of company growth vectors or dimensions.

Has rear-view-mirror mentality.

Resists change and does not keep up with future expectations and trends in the industry, business or geographical theatre or company activities.

Chairman of the board

Honours: Understands and believes in significant difference of roles of chairman (as agent of the board) and chief executive officer (appointed by and responsible to the board), whether both titles are held by one person or by separate persons.

Prepares carefully for meetings.

Gives thoughtful consideration to making meetings the most effective use of time of those assembled.

Insists on reports being properly prepared in advance.

Distinguishes between material for information and material requiring board action.

Keeps discussions on major strategic or policy matters.

Insists on advance review of presentations where appropriate and when needed.

Is competent in chairing and managing group dynamics.

Thoughtful in agenda management.

Considers what executive officers need to focus on at meetings and coaches them on director education and perceptions.

Properly balances exposure of board to advocate and adversary views on major issues.

Encourages constructive debate and independent viewpoints.

Endeavours to make each meeting an interesting and rewarding experience for each participant.

Effective leader with personal respect and established collateral with each member.

Sees that candidates are developed for chairman and CEO succession, whether both titles are held by one or by separate persons.

This involves education and testing process plus understanding of different qualifications for chairmanship and chief executive officer roles.

Pass: Adequate moderator in sum (but not extensive interest or expertise in many considerations above).

Passive interest in facing issues or improving director motivation.

Not forceful leader.

Constructive attitude, but reactive mode.

Chairman of the board (cont.)

Fail: As moderator, acts with little skill, enthusiasm or insight.

Delegates most governance issues to chief executive officer, if the chairman is a non-executive.

Not strong advocate or does not understand (or believe in) explicit separation of roles (even when held by the same person) of chairman and chief executive officer for normal, stabilised corporate situations.

Does little to enable smooth, timely chairman or CEO succession.

Does not effectively encourage discussion.

Is nervous with conflict at meetings.

Wishy-washy attitude on critical issues.

Does not encourage members to contribute to top management in strategy or policy formation.

Does not exercise leadership in motivating directors.

Appendix 2: Twenty-two questions for diagnosing your board

[From W. J. Salmon, 'Crisis Prevention: How to Gear Up Your Board', *Harvard Business Review* (January/February 1993)]

If you answer yes to all 22 questions, you have an exemplary board.

1.   Are there three or more outside directors for every insider?
2.   Are the insiders limited to the CEO, the COO and the CFO?
3.   Do your directors routinely speak to senior managers who are not represented on the board?
4.   Is your board the right size (8 to 15 members)?
5.   Does your audit committee, not management, have the authority to approve the partner in charge of auditing the company?
6.   Does your audit committee routinely review "high-exposure" areas?
7.   Do compensation consultants report to your compensation committee rather than to the company's human resources officers?
8.   Has your compensation committee shown the courage to establish formulas for CEO compensation based on long-term results – even if the formulas differ from industry norms?
9.   Are the activities of your executive committee sufficiently contained to prevent the emergence of a "two-tier" board?
10. Do outside directors annually review succession plans for senior management?

11. Do outside directors formally evaluate your CEO's strengths, weaknesses, objectives, personal plans and performance every year?

12. Does your nominating committee rather than the CEO direct the search for new board members and invite candidates to stand for election?

13. Is there a way for outside directors to alter the meeting agenda set by your CEO?

14. Does the company help directors prepare for meetings by sending relevant routine information, as well as analyses of key agenda items, ahead of time?

15. Is there sufficient meeting time for thoughtful discussion in addition to management monologue?

16. Do the outside directors meet without management on a regular basis?

17. Is your board actively involved in formulating long-range business strategy from the start of the planning cycle?

18. Does your board, rather than the incumbent CEO, select the new chief executive – in fact as well as in theory?

19. Is at least some of directors' pay linked to corporate performance?

20. Is the performance of each of your directors periodically reviewed?

21. Are directors who are no longer pulling their weight discouraged from standing for re-election?

22. Do you take the right measures to build trust among directors?

Appendix 3: Sample diagnostic questions for analysing the board of directors

[From R. F. Lusch and M. G. Harvey, 'The Case for an Off-Balance-Sheet Controller', *Sloan Management Review* (Winter 1994)]

Balance membership

1. Is our board composed of. . .
   a. all inside directors?
   b. one outside director for each inside director?
   c. two outside directors for each inside director?
   d. three or more outside directors?

2. Is our board composed of. . .
   a. directors who have experience only in our industry?
   b. directors who have experience in our industry and related industries?
   c. directors who have experience in our industry, related industries, and unrelated industries.

3. Is our board composed of. . .
   a. directors within ten years of age of each other?
   b. directors within fifteen years of each other?
   c. directors within twenty-five years of each other?

Agenda setting for meetings

4. Is the agenda for our board. . .
    a. set by the CEO?
    b. set by the CEO with input from inside directors?
    c. set by the CEO with input from all directors.

5. Are the agenda and reading materials for our board circulated. . .
    a. one week prior to our meeting?
    b. two weeks prior to our meeting?
    c. three weeks prior to our meeting?

6. Is the typical meeting. . .
    a. so well constructed that there is virtually no time for discussion?
    b. structured so that there is time for brief to moderate discussion of each issue?
    c. structured so that there is time for thoughtful and thorough discussion of the most important issues?

Policy on the election-re-election to board

7. Is the nomination of a new board member handled. . .
    a. totally by the CEO?
    b. by the CEO, who seeks input from all directors?
    c. by a nomination committee with strong input from the CEO?
    d. by the nomination committee with minor input from the CEO?

8. How are board members replaced?
    a. members serve as long as they desire.
    b. members who do not make meetings or otherwise participate are asked to resign or are replaced.
    c. members are formally evaluated each year and replacements are sought as needed.

Operation of committees

9. How does the audit committee operate?
    a. it is told what company will be the auditor.
    b. it is involved in selecting the audit firm.
    c. it recommends to the board which audit firm to use.
    d. it recommends to the board which audit firm to use and approves the audit partner.

10. How does the audit committee establish an agenda?
    a. it is told by the internal auditor what areas to review on an annual basis.
    b. it decides which areas it wishes to investigate.
    c. it decides which areas it wishes to investigate and sets priorities for the study of high exposure areas on a systematic basis.

11. On what does the compensation committee base its compensation recommendations?
    a. on input from the human resource department.
    b. on historical trends and industry practices.
    c. on pre-established standards and a formula-based reward system.

Scoring is done by assigning point values to each answer, such as zero points for (a), one point for (b), two points for (c) and three points for (d). Total scores are evaluated as follows:

0–6   Out of Control. Severe problems exist with the board of directors; the board is probably a liability.

7–14   Losing Control. Serious problems exist with the board of directors; multiple opportunities exist to transform the board into a major asset.

15–20   Partly in Control. The board is generally doing a good job, but a few areas could be improved by taking corrective action.

21–25   In Control. The board is a major asset; it is operating as it should be.

4 The Independent Director and the Investor: New Directions

If capitalism came to an end in 1996, its future historians would no doubt write that, at the level of governance, its last five years were its most tumultuous. We are living in a time of unprecedented upheaval in, or reform of, corporate governance, depending on one's point of view. Around the western world, corporate boards are becoming much more vigorous in exercising their responsibilities. In some well-publicised cases, this has led to open conflict with senior management. Such conflict reflects the increased anxiety many boards are feeling about their companies' stewardship and performance. Reflecting on just one country's recent experience will make the point. Over the past few years, American Express, Citicorp, Digital, General Motors, Goodyear, IBM, Kodak, Sears and Westinghouse have each been subjected to major, independent director-driven upheaval. The directors of these and numerous other corporations have overridden senior executives to demand large-scale reforms, frequently involving a change of CEO. Usually behind such moves has been the increasing restiveness of activist shareholders. It has been said, with some justification, that we have moved from entrepreneurial capitalism to managerial capitalism and now to shareholder capitalism.

In this chapter, we will explore some of these and other trends currently influencing the direction of corporate governance in economies such as ours.

We will also discuss some of the implications of the report of the Committee on the Financial Aspects of Corporate Governance (the Cadbury Report). Many are, or will be, of supreme importance for the future structure and practices of our boards. We shall examine in turn current developments in shareholder–board relationships, board–management relationships, and board structures and practices, and the fundamental contribution that the independent director can make to each of these developments.

Shareholder–board relationships

In the light of the events described above, there is no doubt that institutional investors have forced the spotlight to be shone brightly on this relationship. Especially in North America, it is now accepted that big investors would not be meeting their obligations to their members if they were to ignore the under-performance of a firm in which they had a significant stake.

Influence

Too often the public impression given of this development is a false one. There is a tendency to characterise large shareholders as Wild West figures, riding roughshod over boards who have a much broader constituency, and a more intimate company knowledge, than those shareholders. The reality, in our view, is different, and much more positive. The increasing tendency, as our survey confirms, is for such investors to attempt to alert boards to what they perceive as areas of actual or potential under-performance. At the same time, as opposed to a decade ago, most are now concerned to advise those firms of their desire to stay for the long haul. Their focus is on engaging with boards to add sustainable value to the firm. There is no doubt that activist institutional shareholders have been instrumental in the trend towards clarifying the distinctive roles of (especially independent) directors and managers. They have also driven the increasing emphasis on non-executive board members taking the lead role in selecting, compensating and overseeing senior executives. In general, the thrust is one of clarifying for board members that their primary responsibility is not to the senior executives, but to the owners.

Within this general trend, however, there are several variations. Some institutional shareholders are in fact not at all concerned about selecting directors. Some are not particularly concerned about the direction taken by a company in which they have a stake. Such investors *are*, however, concerned to know that there *is* an agreed direction, and that its success, or lack of success, is being closely scrutinised by the board and particularly its independent members. For many years now, of course, large institutional shareholders have had extraordinarily elaborate methodologies and systems for analysing corporate performance. While these are becoming more complex and sophisticated, the ways in which their results are being used are becoming much more subtle. Increasingly, the objective is to understand the organisational mind-set of an under-performing company and to ask whether or not the board genuinely grasps the need for new approaches: whether it is proactively striking out in new directions, or simply reacting crudely to each new set of bad numbers. Clearly, large shareholders themselves are these days much more proactive. They are keen to have a disciplined method for identifying and addressing possible trouble spots. Increasingly, they are seeking to turn under-performers around, rather than abandon them.

United States

In the United States, a significant regulatory change came into effect in 1992. These were the new Securities and Exchange Commission rules that loosened the prohibition on one investor exchanging information with another. The jury is still out on this reform. Its supporters argue that greater exchanges between investors, and between boards and investors, will have the effect of exercising the same market disciplines that were enforced by the possibility of acquisition in the 1980s. They claim that, since it is now legally possible for one sizable investor to contact others and seek information about a particular company, there is now much more of a genuine exchange on, and market for, improved corporate performance. Indeed, they include in this 'exchange' not just analysts and investment managers, but also members of corporate boards. The reform's opponents – who, interestingly, do include some substantial institutional investors – worry that 'communication' might become something more than that: it might turn into concerted deeds, not merely the exchange of words and data. They fear that the collective power of a few large shareholders could have a corrupting effect.

We shall have to wait and see on this one. For economies such as ours, the intriguing thing about that particular reform is that it is symptomatic of an international regulatory and legislative trend towards increasing, on the one hand, the freedom and power of the investor and, on the other, the accountability of the director. Another recent trend has been the advocacy by some large shareholders – usually public funds rather than private fund management companies – of 'shareholders' advisory committees'. The claim that these are necessary is based on the view that boards have many concerns, only one of which is share value. Therefore, it is argued, there is a need for another layer of scrutiny to focus exclusively on that issue. Typically, the argument is that that layer should be peopled only by direct representatives of the firm's largest shareholders. We *are* prepared to make a prediction about this one. Our prediction is that it will die a deserved and relatively speedy death. The logic behind this proposal is, shall we say, not obvious. Such committees could be extremely active. In which case, they would undermine the board/management relationship, with dysfunctional consequences for the firm's operations and therefore, ultimately, a negative impact on share price.

Alternatively, such a committee – having noted these negative consequences of activism – could do very little. In which case, the committee's necessity would be called into question. In either scenario, it is hard to foresee a shareholders' advisory committee meeting the objective set for it by its advocates, namely, increasing the value of investors' holdings. It is, in our view, an idea with a great future behind it.

Asset appropriateness

Another trend among large shareholders is likely to have more staying power. This is their increasing demand that boards focus on asset *appropriateness*, rather than asset *size*. Over the past few years, there has been a discernible change in shareholder philosophy on this point. Large investors are now much less interested in the question of firm size. The tendency now is to regard appropriate firm size to be the logical outcome of a disciplined focus on capacity to produce sustainably high levels of ROE. This change is in part a product of broader macroeconomic changes. In times of price volatility, asset acquisition has a good deal to recommend it: inflation will do the job of asset revaluation for you. In times of relative price stability, such as we look like enjoying at least for the medium term, the central concern is: does the firm possess the *appropriate* assets for producing those levels of Return on Equity (ROE)?

A good deal of effort has been expended by large shareholders in recent times to persuade boards to think in these terms: appropriateness (in ROE terms) of asset base and efficient allocation of capital. The intriguing difference here – as with several of the developments we have described so far – is between public funds and private fund management companies. In general, the large public funds seek to ensure that directors have and exercise the appropriate degree of responsibility to carry out their traditionally assigned duties – setting a framework for the firm, monitoring firm performance, and selection and dismissal of the CEO.

These investors typically wish directors – particularly independent directors – to conduct performance analysis on their behalf. The less publicised players in the field of increased shareholder activism have been the large private fund managers. They tend to take the view that they, unlike public funds, *do* have the capacity to make judgements about management performance. When they observe what they take to be management of companies with a shareholder orientation, increasingly they are taking quite significant holdings in those companies.

This focus on management orientation and performance may well have serious implications for corporate governance if it has the effect of investors dealing directly with – and, in a sense, *investing in* – company management. If the board truly is the agent of the investors, then it is hard to see how it can effectively prosecute that role in these sorts of circumstances. This is a trend well worth watching in the immediate future. It is not to be confused with the last of the recent developments that we wish to deal with: a development that has come to be known as 'Relationship Investing'.

Relationship investing

It is hard to capture neatly all the different arrangements encompassed by this term, but each arrangement certainly involves a long-term, committed relationship between investors and a firm. At one extreme so far, it has involved shareholders taking not only seats on boards, but also some leverage on behalf of the investee firm. At its other extreme, it involves no more than regular shareholder–board meetings. Typically, the focus is on under-performing companies. The relationship investor acquires a sizable chunk of shares, takes a board seat and sets about giving advice aimed at lifting corporate performance over the medium term.

Its supporters claim that this is one of the greatest benefits of relationship investing: it is not driven by collapsed timeframes. Relationship investors' funds, it is said, are enduring and therefore liberate directors and managers to concentrate on sustainable value over the long haul. From the shareholders' viewpoint, energetic scrutiny of their stocks' performance creates an extra dimension of corporate liability. (Of course, neither of these 'benefits' would be particularly newsworthy in corporate environments such as Germany or Japan. In such systems, it has been standard practice at least since the Second World War for significant investors to consciously acquire enduring shares in companies along with directorships on these companies' higher boards.) It is, nevertheless, apparent that shareholder-led restructures have increased the share price of several firms, which is presumably, at least in part, a positive comment by the market on these firms' likely performances over the long haul. US examples include Allied Signal, Avon, General Motors, Goodyear, Kodak, Lockheed, Sears and Tenneco. In the words of a partner in one of the leading relationship investors: 'Corporate governance is our tool for making money. We are talking about non takeover takeovers. Like the raiders, we hope to realise value that's buried. We've found a better, earlier way to do it.'

So far, relationship investing seems to have the numbers on its side. Over the past five years, stock of US companies in which relationship investors have taken a position has beaten Standard-and-Poor's 500-stock index by an average 30 points. These investor firms have different approaches to relationship investing. Some buy friendly stakes in companies that have begun to change for the better, but need to buy more time to do so. An investor representative takes a board seat. Others buy large negotiated stakes in firms that require fresh capital. In order to influence corporate policies and monitor management, the investor takes at least one seat on the board each time. Others again invest in poorly performing firms. They contact management and try through negotiation with the chair to redirect strategy.

In brief, the argument for relationship investing is that investors who thoroughly understand a firm's direction, why it is the most appropriate of the options available, and who do so without an intervening layer of brokers and analysts, are more likely to stay with the firm over the long haul. It becomes a more effective method for firms to manage expectations. What is ignored by the arguments in favour, of course, is that, from a corporate board's viewpoint, the value of a relationship rather depends on the other half of that relationship. Few of the benefits described above will accrue to a company with a 10 per cent shareholder who, without actually making any value-added contribution, still demands to be consulted constantly. It is possible to imagine situations in which such investors would seek to monitor every operational decision – which would lead to a great deal of company–investor interaction but very little else. Moreover, although there is little hard evidence of this so far, it is not inconceivable that this new kind of investment could in some cases increase a focus on the near term. Directors who felt that their every move was being monitored by a large shareholder could become significantly more risk-averse and seek to ring up immediate 'runs on the board'.

Shareholder activism

To repeat, the figures so far do seem to provide support for this more positive style of relationship investing. A limitation on the validity of these figures, however, is that so far this trend has largely been confined to the US. Shareholder activism is certainly on the rise in other countries, but there is little evidence thus far in these countries of the long-term negotiated position-taking outlined above. We shall mention briefly some other recent international developments.

- In mid-1992, it was announced that Andrew Buxton would become chairman and chief executive of Barclays Bank on 1 January 1993. In December, non-executive board members, having consulted with large investors, decided that given the bank's declining earnings and growing bad debts, it would be prudent to separate the roles and appoint an outside chief executive.
- In the past few years, agitation by investors has led to the departure of senior management at many large UK firms, such as British Aerospace and Burton Group.
- In 1992, the Cadbury Report on corporate governance was released in Britain. It codified 'best corporate governance practice', recommending dividing the positions of chief executive and chairman, increasing the power of Non Executive Directors on compensation and audit committees, and disclosing senior management compensation more fully. The biggest immediate effect of the report was greatly to raise public consciousness of corporate governance issues. It has, however, met significant resistance to some of its proposals.
- An increasing number of shareholders are successfully seeking board representation. Two of the more public battles, resolved in the shareholders' favour, were at WPP Group plc and Teledanmark, the Danish telecommunications giant.
- Fund managers in individual European countries are tending to share information and investment strategies with their opposite numbers in other countries to a much greater extent than ever before.
- Shareholders have succeeded in forcing Nestlé to open its registered shares to foreign holders.
- The Japanese Justice Ministry has made changes to the commercial code to force firms to take on truly independent auditors and to make it legally easier for shareholders to sue directors.

- Perhaps most significantly, CALPERS has launched an international governance programme, targeting specific companies in the UK, France and Japan.

We have touched only lightly on these developments. There are hundreds more, from the past twelve months alone. What they amount to is a consistent trend, worldwide, toward greater activism by, and power of, shareholders. Outside the US, it is still at a relatively less developed, but more aggressive, stage. Within the US, where the movement has a longer history, the advent of relationship investing raises the prospect of a more constructive – but no less demanding – future for the director/ shareholder relationship.

Director–manager relationships

Discussions about the appropriate relationship between board and management will be familiar to most of our readers, and we will not rehearse them. What we will try to do is to give a brief overview of recent international developments within the context of these discussions. Clearly, the most dramatic of those developments has been the board dismissal of several chief executives of very large corporations. When, for example, on 6 April 1992, the non-executive directors of General Motors restructured the composition of the company's senior management, they shed light on an entirely new dimension to the board/management relationship.

This dramatic event was symptomatic of a trend for boards to be more activist in the prosecution of their traditional role, but also to query some aspects of that role. One of the most common reactions to the General Motors events was to question why the board had not taken action sooner. (This same reaction was produced by virtually all of the board-led changes mentioned at the beginning of this chapter.) For the first time, there is now genuine debate about the merits or otherwise of combining the roles of CEO and Chair; about appropriate responsibility for setting board agendas; about appropriate responsibility for assigning work to board committees; about retaining former CEOs as board members; and about permitting CEOs a role in choosing their successors. We shall not deal with each of these issues, but concentrate on those that are central, as well, to the issues arising from the Cadbury Report. Of these, without question, the most pressing currently is that of the role of the independent director.

Independent director

We use the term 'independent director' advisedly. A good deal of the post-Cadbury debate has been about 'non-executive directors', when what has actually been intended is a sub-category of them, namely individuals chosen for the board with *no* other connection with the firm, be it employee, investor, customer or supplier. In the light of Cadbury, it is fair to say that a major focus of attention will be the concept of the 'unitary board', and whether the Cadbury recommendations concerning independent directors undermine that concept. Cadbury highlights a monitoring responsibility for independent directors, stating that they should appoint a leader on each board and that 'NEDs are in the best position to monitor the performance of the board and that of the chief executive'. The report further suggests that only independent directors should have access to independent professional advice at the firm's expense and that the chairs of the audit and remuneration committees should be responsible for answering questions at the annual general meeting. Unsurprisingly, these recommendations have aroused considerable debate. We believe that that debate is central to the medium-term future of the director–management relationship.

The unitary board is a fact of life for virtually all public and private companies in economies such as Britain, New Zealand and Australia. It sets obligations in law on every board member for the governance of the firm. Both categories of board member are responsible for safeguarding the investors' welfare. Many have seen a possible danger in the Cadbury suggestions, namely, that they ignore this shared legal responsibility and would tend to set one category of director against another. A further danger is that executive board members might come to see the monitoring role as purely a job for their independent colleagues. This, of course, could lead to a weakening of the notion that a board is a team all of whose members share responsibility. The great threat in all this is the possible outbreak of battles between executive and independent directors over 'their' patches. At the heart of this problem is the issue of whether independent directors are supposed to be monitors *only*, or should be drawing on their skills and backgrounds to progress the company generally. This is central to current developments in the board/management relationship. Survey after survey of CEOs reveals that the characteristics rated most highly in independent directors by chief executives are business experience and knowledge.

Assuming that independent directors will increasingly be chosen for the breadth of experience and skills that they can bring to a board, then there is a serious question about the appropriateness of limiting their contribution to that of a monitoring role. To deny such directors the opportunity to exploit their backgrounds by contributing to setting the policy framework would be rather self-defeating. Now, it can safely be assumed that none of this was *intended* by the Cadbury Committee. As in many spheres of life, however, we are in an area where perception is more powerful than reality. And a widely held perception is that the scenario we have outlined is the logical outcome of the Cadbury proposals. In any event, it is certainly true to say that the major contemporary development in this area of board–management relationships is deep and active consideration of the size of the board's 'portfolio' – monitor, adviser, or both? A very great deal of debate is occurring on boards on how many of the following activities are their appropriate responsibilities:

1. Monitoring management performance
2. Ensuring legal compliance
3. Ensuring ethical behaviour
4. Developing strategy
5. Monitoring strategy implementation
6. Signing off on key strategic decisions.

Information for the board

The other significant recent development in this area that we wish to touch on are new trends in the provision of information to the board. There has recently been a considerable concentration on effective information flows to boards. This is a product of the fact that directors are increasingly required to understand not only their own organisation, but also its industry, its competitive environment, prospective management successions, and its short, medium, and long-term strategies. Behind all this are the increasingly taxing legal obligations on directors, making possession of the appropriate information an absolute imperative. In large measure, of course, it is management who provides that information. In a recent survey of corporate board practices by Korn/ Ferry International, 300 leading CEOs said that the five areas that their boards were most concerned about were; maximising shareholder value, financial results, management succession, strategic planning, and long-term survival. No other issue ranked close to these. There is no doubt that information flow to boards is now increasingly reflecting – indeed, is being driven by – these areas that boards themselves are most focused on.

An important development here, consistent with this trend, is the provision of *both* current operating financial data *and* material that deals with the company's strategic plans. There also seems to be a trend toward provision of board papers that are *uniquely* 'board papers' – not simply material produced already for management and reproduced in precisely the same form for the board. Rather, the trend, certainly in larger companies – again, driven by the *board's* priority concerns – is to reformulate and summarise management data according to categories determined by the board. Another development is the trend toward provision of competitor analyses. Increasingly, as the competitor intelligence function becomes more sophisticated, boards are being presented with comparisons of their company's current performance with those of their competitors. The provision of 'CEO time' is another recent trend. This is something different from, and additional to, the CEO's formal report. It is a portion of time set aside – typically near the conclusion of a full board meeting – for a relatively informal and interactive session in which the CEO expresses his/her views on a range of issues and engages with directors (sometimes with the independent directors only) in a 'without prejudice' suggestion-and-question session.

One further recent trend concerns the issue of sensitivity to inside information. Many boards are now using window periods with regard to the purchase and sale of shares, in order to protect board members from claims about their possessing inside information. There is also an increasing tendency for new independent directors to be put on a 'briefing and breaking in' programme (the phrase is employed by the Board of Koppers Co.). This, usually a six–eight week schedule, involves taking the new director around major company facilities, meeting unit or departmental managers, being briefed on the industry and competition, and generally giving him/her as deep a feel as is possible in that period for the firm and its environment. Beyond this, boards overseas are tending to want to have a regular programme of this kind – for the board as a whole, irrespective of individual members' length of company experience. Bulova is one corporation that has been at the forefront of this trend. A further development is for independent board members with particularly strong expertise in certain business disciplines – marketing, finance, etc. – to have regular 'without prejudice' discussions with senior company personnel in those areas.

We conclude this section with some predictions about a number of other current 'hot' topics in this area. Three suggestions being put about with some frequency currently are: creating shareholder committees to monitor management's performance; requiring the board to enter its own separate report in the company's annual report; and creating a 'lead' independent director with special responsibility for monitoring management's performance against plan. Our prediction is, that, in five years' time, we will be able to look back and gratefully note the unlamented death of these less than brilliant schemes.

Director selection

A quite noticeable international trend in recent times has been the adoption of more formal and rigourous director selection procedures. Many more boards than in years gone by are actually *planning* their composition, with the company's strategic goals in mind. From this starting point, the specifications of the most appropriate board *mix* are drawn up. These serve as guidelines for the director selection process.

Increasingly, too, specifications for *individual* board positions are being drawn up and used as guides in that process. Greater attention is being given to staggering the ages of new directors, so that, in turn, retirement dates are staggered. This prevents the loss at one stroke of large chunks of the board's collective knowledge. Formal position descriptions for boards are increasingly in use, and it is becoming very common for the whole process of director selection to be driven by a nominating committee composed of independent directors. Certainly in North America, and increasingly in Europe, the nominating committee engages the services of a search firm – the 'big six' international search firms all now have specialist board practices – or the director selection arm of the local Institute of Directors. All of this is a good deal more costly, in both money and time, than traditional, more informal methods. Given the numbers of boards adopting and staying with this approach, it can only be assumed that these are costs worth incurring. Further refinements are the more elaborate briefings that prospective candidates are now being given, concerning the time expectations, standards of performance, committee assignments and workloads, and preparation requirements.

We have already mentioned some of the current processes of inducting new directors. This is increasingly being taken as a responsibility of the board as a whole, on the understanding that it should be a *planned* process, aimed at bringing new members up to speed as quickly as possible. The process increasingly includes meetings with significant investors, in addition to the activities that I have already described. This raises one final point about selection. There is doubt that the nominating committee has been one of the most significant developments in corporate governance in recent times. It is now widely acknowledged as *the* critical board committee and the key to sound corporate governance. What is in dispute is whether its membership should include the major shareholder, or its nominations should be subject to veto by the major shareholder, or that shareholder should have only an informal, and consultative role in the selection process, or none at all. Practice currently diverges widely on this question, which we suspect will be put under an increasingly bright glare in the years ahead.

5   Dealing with the Unexpected: The Board of Directors and Takeovers

Introduction

Ever since Berle and Means, in their famous work *The Modern Corporation and Private Property* (1934), documented the problems relating to the separation of ownership and control in business, corporate governance practitioners and students have been concerned with the issue of managerialism. Berle and Means suggested that the diffusion of share ownership was one of the main reasons for the increasing influence of managerialism. As shareholders are diffused, they argued, the likelihood of co-ordinated action by shareholders declines.

In more recent times, however, this debate has been refocused by the rise in influence of institutional investors. Shareholder activism, spearheaded by co-ordinating bodies such as the Council for Institutional Investors in the United States, has created greater pressure on management to be accountable to their shareholders. Increased concentration of a company's share ownership in the hands of a small number of institutions gives those institutions significant voting power that can have the effect of reducing management influence on matters requiring board-level decisions. Perhaps more important is the *implicit* power that large shareholders exert on issues such as executive compensation and executive control. Much of this implicit power derives simply from the size of their equity holdings: heavy institutional selling can cause steep declines in a firm's market value.

This growing force in the market has introduced a new dynamic to the corporate control debate. This chapter will explore some of the features of that new dynamic. We shall focus particularly on the question of anti-takeover devices, because it is only in decision situations involving a conflict of interest between management and shareholders that the effectiveness of the board's intervention can be assessed accurately. In other cases, so long as the interests of management and shareholders coincide, any type of board, even a passive one, will appear to be an effective corporate governance institution.

We will explore the question of what it is that institutional investors want from an investment. When does an institutional investor consider the takeover of a company that it 'owns' to be a good thing or a bad thing? And how should such an investor view any anti-takeover amendments proposed by the board of the company in which it has a major shareholding?

Institutional shareholders will view a takeover offer from three perspectives. The first two are more important and address long-term value creation. The third is more short-term but will sometimes influence fund managers who are attracted by the benefit to their portfolio of short-term gains. The three perspectives are:

1. Will the merged company provide greater total returns over time, adjusted for the time value of cash flow? The answer will be based on strategic worth, financial strength and synergy from the merger.
2. Will the new management be more capable of delivering the benefits that the old management has not been able to do?

Both of these questions are core to long-term value creation.

3. Does the proposed acquisition give a cash alternative that is significantly in excess of the target company's stand-alone share price, using 'normal' valuation criteria?

The debate on these issues ranges around a number of arguments. Principal among these is the 'managerialist' argument, namely, that managers come to their roles with a wide portfolio of personal objectives relating to compensation, continued employment, personal status and maintaining their positions of control. This argument holds that management will often, in the natural order of events, pursue different strategies from those designed to maximise shareholder value.

The counter view is put by the 'stewardship' argument, which, crudely stated, says: 'Let the manager manage'. This argument contends that managers are hired to manage, trained to manage and selected specifically to do a certain job, which they can do far better than fund managers or investment analysts whose expertise is of a completely different kind. Proponents of this argument also contend that there are sufficient checks and balances embodied in different institutions of capitalism to keep management honest, and alert to the interests of all stakeholders.

A third view, the 'shareholder interests' argument, contends that, in a takeover situation, it is good for the board of the target company to be in as powerful a position as possible in order to maximise takeover synergies for their shareholders (in other words, ensure the highest attainable price).

In what follows, we shall consider the interplay of these arguments, testing them on the specific question of anti-takeover amendments, and bring to bear some recent evidence in this vexed area. The framework question for our analysis is: How should the board respond when it receives a takeover bid?

We have two starting points for our discussion. The first is that it is a normal part of good housekeeping for a board to consider its and the company's preparedness to face a potential bid. This should include an ongoing consideration of what needs to be addressed in order to maximise shareholder value. It should also include an up-to-date knowledge of the share register, and an assurance that all appropriate Section 212 notices have been sent out regularly. Our second starting point is that, as we have indicated in Chapters 1 and 2, the board must act in the interests of all shareholders and not of specific groups.

Institutional investors

Over the past fifty years, the share market has witnessed a shift towards increased institutional ownership. From a relatively low point in the late 1940s, we have come to a position in the 1990s in which institutional funds control almost a majority of the shares held in major corporations. In the United States, for example, institutional holdings of US corporations has grown from 40 per cent of common stock in 1949 to over 50 per cent in many industries today. This has resulted in part from a growth in public and private pension and retirement funds.

The policy of institutional investors is generally to invest in companies or sectors which they see as offering sustained above-market-average growth, in terms of total return. It is often said that one of the main reasons for institutional funds targeting the corporate sector is a desire for a higher return than they can get from other investments. Poor interest rates on bonds and from banks is linked with the institutional investors' move to the corporate sector. They are investing in companies which can provide them with a good return, particularly those whose stock has been under-priced, and in which they see possibilities of improved corporate performance. If the company does not perform as well as expected, the institutional investors can exert pressure through their large shareholdings for actions to be taken that are likely to improve earnings. Some observers have even suggested that large investors would go so far as to mount takeover bids in order to improve their company's performance.

Not only are institutional shareholders buying a larger number of shares than in earlier eras. Their portfolios are also more diversified than before. Some institutional funds have upwards of a hundred different company holdings in their portfolios. Their high equity positions in individual companies, plus their general portfolio diversity, allow institutional investors to support the reduced use of anti-takeover devices. This is because the institutions have diversified their risk and are now not as vulnerable to the under-performance of an individual company. This was borne out by a survey of institutional investors as long ago as 1987, in which 81 per cent of respondents said that they did not support the use of anti-takeover devices. Having diversified, and thus reduced their risk, institutions may see such devices as standing in the way of improved company performance. No longer too worried about individual company protection, they are more concerned with returns on their investments.

Institutional investors are often accused of increasing managerial risk-aversion because, it is said, institutional money-managers emphasise short-term gains while managing investment portfolios. Critics attribute fund managers' pursuits of short-term returns to the fact that their personal rewards are based on quarterly or annual results.

We feel that this alleged managerial risk-aversion is an oversimplification of what is in fact a more complex issue. Institutional investors possess a unique set of characteristics which qualify their investment decisions. By holding diversified portfolios, institutional investors are able to diversify their exposure to risk and are consequently attracted to high risk/high return strategies pursued by individual companies within their portfolios. Institutional investors also have unique characteristics relating to exit. They find it difficult to sell large blocks of shares without significantly depressing the share price. This being the case, they tend to retain the holding and attempt to 'wake up' the board and management of an under-performing company, arguing for a better return on investment and threatening more overt shareholder action. Additionally, it is clear that institutions will migrate towards investments which offer sustained growth potential. The research of Rechner suggests that institutional investors value capital investment in longer-term projects. This observation is consistent with the finding that firms experience an upturn in their market value on announcing an increase in R&D expenditure, typically an indication of long-termism. It is consistent as well with our own findings (see Chapter 1) that institutions do, in fact, tend to take a long-term view when assessing companies' prospects.

Institutional investors have put pressure on boards to set up compensation packages for directors which contain greater stock ownership characteristics. These stock ownership packages tie the directors' and boards' performance directly to their compensation, thus making the board more responsive to the market and investors. This is thought to be another reason for institutional investors not supporting anti-takeover devices.

Clearly, institutional investors believe that board composition is an important factor affecting company performance. As a result, they seek increased outside representation on boards. This, they believe, improves the board's effectiveness in being more responsive to shareholders and improves the overall corporate performance. With the greater proportion of corporate ownership in the hands of institutional investors, these kinds of changes are beginning to emerge throughout the corporate world.

Institutional investors and takeovers

Naturally, institutional investors are interested primarily in the financial performance of their investments. In this light, they view the market for corporate control as a mechanism for disciplining under-performing boards and managers, and for reducing the negative effects on shareholders' wealth of such under-performance and/or poor communication by managers and boards. This is because prolonged managerial inefficiency is most likely to initiate a downward trend in the firm's share price. The resulting under-evaluation of the company's shares makes it an attractive target for takeovers and hence jeopardises management's control position but increases the likelihood of good returns for the institutional investor. Kesner and Dalton have shown that the common share price of a takeover target increases by approximately 30 per cent if the takeover is successful, and actually declines by a small percentage if the attempt is unsuccessful.

A common situation faced by institutional investors in under-performing companies can be illustrated as follows:

- An institution has a large shareholding in a company.
- The company gives no indication of turning around, despite shareholder activism on the part of the institution.
- The institution would have difficulty in selling a large holding without further depressing the share price.

In such a case, the institutional investor would wish to maximise its takeover-related gains if a bid were made by a third party. Would any known anti-takeover devices assist institutional investors to do this, or would they frustrate the whole process by deterring all potential takeover bids? We shall address this question later in this chapter by considering five anti-takeover mechanisms in detail. First we shall briefly rehearse in more depth the issues raised in the introduction to the chapter.

The arguments

Anti-takeover devices are often the most debated issues on the agendas of annual general meetings. Increasing numbers of institutional investors are departing from the traditional Wall Street Rule voting against anti-takeover amendments.

Shareholder interests

Why all the debate? Followers of the shareholder interests argument claim that the adoption of anti-takeover mechanisms actually increases current shareholder wealth. They argue that management teams should always adopt such mechanisms for two reasons:

- The adoption of these amendments would create in effect a long-term contract between shareholders and the current management team. It may encourage long-term investment and retention of earnings to pursue growth opportunities, which are in the best interests of the shareholders.
- Such devices give target management additional negotiating leverage or veto power, enabling them to negotiate better deals on average for their shareholders.

The argument runs that shareholders can maximise their potential takeover-related gains by adopting anti-takeover mechanisms and awarding management a golden parachute of the optimal size. We believe, however, that anything that inhibits shareholders exercising their rights to vote on a company's future is, in fact, counterproductive and likely to reduce value. The recent British case of the Forte 'golden share' vote on Granada's takeover offer is a good example.

Stewardship

Proponents of the stewardship argument claim that the socialisation process during the careers of top managers, and the degree of mutual monitoring practised among managers, work to keep them focused on the goal of maximising the firm's value. They also contend that there are any number of 'institutions of capitalism' which counter any tendency towards managerial entrenchment and help to keep management performing efficiently. These include:

- the market for corporate control
- competitive forces in the product market
- outside directors
- separation of the CEO and Chair functions
- performance-based compensation
- equity ownership by management
- the external labour market for managers
- internal labour and capital markets
- concentrated ownership
- increased institutional shareholder activism
- choice of financial structure, including debt and dividend policies.

Managerialism

On the other hand, proponents of the managerialist argument counter that these institutions of capitalism serve to attenuate, not eliminate, managerial discretion. They claim that anti-takeover mechanisms reduce the effectiveness of the market for corporate control and therefore exacerbate the problem of managerial entrenchment. The majority of shareholders of a given company may well be rationally ignorant (uninformed), and therefore vote to put in place devices that are not actually in their best interests. The institutional investor, on the recommendation of management, may well follow suit.

Stakeholders

The other major view in this area is that the shareholder is not the only stakeholder, and that the job of management is to 'satisfice' between the competing claims of all stakeholders, optimising for none but sufficing for all. Proponents of this view hold that the fiduciary obligations of both managers and directors is solely to 'the company'. Hence their hands should be freed in order to balance these commitments, to buffer the organisation by maintaining some under-utilised resources, and to serve the interests of the organisation as a 'going concern', even if these come at the expense of shareholder wealth.

Institutional investors, while possibly sympathising with the difficult job of management, would nevertheless insist on their right to a competitive return on their investment. They could suggest that, especially in the context of anti-takeover mechanisms, the stakeholder view is little more than an excuse for inefficiency and under-performance.

Our summary opinion of this view is that, while in law the board has a duty to make a judgement in shareholders' interests, in practice things are not so clear cut. The reality is that regard does need to be paid to other interests. Perhaps this can be expressed as: maximising shareholder value subject to specific minimum constraints!

Anti-takeover amendments

We shall now consider five anti-takeover devices in a little detail. We have chosen these five because they illustrate an interesting gradation in terms of their usefulness to the institutional investor, and because they allow us to illustrate critically the central themes of this chapter.

Greenmail

One of the most costly anti-takeover mechanisms is greenmail, which is largely a North American phenomenon. In this case, a buyer obtains a substantial block of a company's shares and then threatens a tender offer. Management, concerned about losing control, buys out the would-be acquirer at a premium. In the United States, corporate raiders are known to seek out greenmail targets systematically and threaten a hostile takeover in the expectation of being greenmailed, when they in fact have no intention of mounting a serious takeover.

Greenmail allows incumbent management to consolidate its control position and to shield itself from the disciplining influence of the market for corporate control. It is therefore likely to be the 'thin edge of the wedge', since it makes it easier for further opportunistic and self-indulgent managerial behaviour to be engaged in at shareholders' expense. Succumbing to greenmail in the first instance cues other raiders to the company's vulnerability and encourages them to engage in further hostile activities. Some companies use the greenmail strategy even when no explicit takeover attempt has been made, or where the potential threat is not very credible. In these instances, greenmail is a clear indication of managerial entrenchment at the expense of the shareholders.

If the target company finances the share repurchase through debt, this may be reflected in reduced dividend payments or higher risk of corporate default, which lowers the value of the firm's share price and decreases the value of future investment opportunities for the shareholders. The extra money paid to the raider disappears from the corporation, for no extra value to the institutional investor, who would have stood to gain, perhaps substantially, had the takeover gone ahead.

The evidence is clear that greenmail transactions which are successful in fending off takeover attempts negatively affect the value of the firm via a significant drop in the company's average returns. Companies that resist greenmail have 'more outside directors, more directors with executive experience, and more directors who represent inter-organisational transactions than boards of companies that paid greenmail' (Mallette and Fowler).

From the perspective of the institutional investor in the target firm, greenmail amendment proposals should always be opposed in the most vigorous terms. We believe that greenmail is usually indefensible and undesirable if the key objective of the board is to maximise shareholder value.

The poison pill

A poison pill is enacted when the board of a company declares a dividend of one share purchase right for each outstanding common share. This right has no economic value until a raider acquires a nominated percentage of the company's shares without board approval. When this occurs, all other shareholders are able to use the right to purchase additional shares at a sizeable discount to market price. This inflicts a level of dilution on both the voting power and economic value of the company's stock that raiders will find unacceptable. It is therefore an extremely effective means of negating any possibility of a hostile takeover.

Institutional investors dislike all anti-takeover devices, and the poison pill is no exception. 'Poison pills strengthen management's control of a firm, decrease shareholder wealth, and deter takeover bids that may result in significant shareholder gain. They represent a clear conflict of shareholders' and managers' interests' (Mallette and Fowler).

This is the main reason for institutional investors seeking more non-executive directors on boards of companies in which they invest. It is preferable, they believe, that the directors have a high stock ownership in the company. If this is the case, some institutional investors believe that the directors will be more responsive to their wishes. There is evidence however, that NEDs' having high ownership in the company has no bearing as to whether or not a poison pill is implemented. On the other hand, the amount of ownership by executive directors does have a significant bearing on the adoption of the pill. The more ownership that executive directors have in a company, the less likely they are to pass the pill. Evidence also shows that the greater the degree of institutional investment in a company the less likely it is that a poison pill will be implemented.

In another respect, there does seem to be a direct correlation between board structure and use of the pill. This was borne out in a recent survey of over 600 companies, of which 226 had the poison pill and 447 did not. The study showed that only 26 of those 226 companies had split the roles of CEO and board chairman. Irrespective of the sympathy of the non-executive directors for the institutional shareholders, 'a powerful CEO-chairperson may be able to push a poison pill through the adoption process regardless of the percentage of independent directors on a board' (Mallette and Fowler).

Generally, a poison pill is truly poisonous to the aspirations of the institutional investor, which would wish to maximise its takeover-related gains. Moreover, if a poison pill is enacted, then anti-takeover power will become entrenched with the board. For this reason, an institutional investor in such a company, when faced with a proposal to implement a poison pill, should oppose it.

Golden parachutes

The golden parachute is a large payment guaranteed to directors and senior management who are rationalised in the course of a takeover. It has been suggested that golden parachutes should be viewed as contingent compensation contracts for top managers to help align directors' interests with those of the shareholders. Such contingent compensation, it is sometimes argued, diminishes the conflict between top management's personal interests and shareholders' interests. Indeed, from this perspective, if a contract is optimally devised, it may motivate management not to resist a legitimate attempt by another, better equipped management team to obtain control of the firm.

Firms with undervalued share prices may find it difficult to recruit and secure directors or senior executives of sufficiently high calibre without offering some sort of golden parachute compensation package. Critics of golden parachutes call them 'rewards for failure' and 'insurance against incompetence'. They feel that managers should be rewarded for their good performance and not compensated for poor performance.

The adoption of a golden parachute is said to alert the market that the company has an increased chance of being the subject of a takeover bid. This does not mean that the tender offer will be successful, that the shareholders and managers will be aligned or that inefficient managers will become entrenched. It does indicate, however, that the individuals on a board will now benefit from a takeover much more than they would have done previously. Investors have a right to be fearful of the golden parachute, since their interests and those of the board may now differ.

Managers are paid to look after the best interests of the shareholders. Why should they require additional inducements to align themselves with those interests? Perhaps the strongest argument against golden parachutes is that many of these contract agreements are initiated after the threat of a takeover has already been identified. The decision that investors face in such cases is a matter of very fine judgement:

- Would the directors resist a potentially lucrative (to the shareholders) bid, or would they perceive that their first obligation was to the shareholders?
- Would a golden parachute of the optimal size induce them to take the desired action?
- If they resisted the bid but failed, would they simply pocket a large stipend for nothing except being in the right place at the right time?
- Would the post-takeover share price increase cover the extra compensation payments?
- Would the extra cost deter one, or a number of, takeover bids?

One recent study found that neither the existence nor the size of a CEO's golden parachute had any significant effect on the likelihood that a target firm would resist a tender offer. It found, however, that stock options do tend to have such an effect (Buchholtz and Ribbens). We contend that in general the institutional investor should oppose golden parachute compensation provisions as a form of 'feather-bedding', and that they should apprise directors of their obligations.

Classified board provisions

When employing this anti-takeover strategy, a company modifies its constitution to stagger the terms of office of its directors and eliminates the mandatory retirement age. When directors' terms expire at varying times, it is difficult for raiders to mount a quick contest for corporate control.

On the one hand, there are some grounds for arguing for a classified board provision. It is clear that an inefficient 'rush' by individual shareholders to tender at an early-offered bid price would be less than optimal for the institutional shareholder. One possible way to counteract this inefficiency is to force the bidding firm to deal directly with the board of directors of the target firm. The target firm's board should be able to collude more effectively than could individual shareholders. Therefore, adopting a classified board would force the bidding firm to deal with a small, cohesive group. This may result in better managed negotiation of the takeover share price, and higher return to all shareholders, institutional and individual alike.

On the other hand, just as for raiders, classified board provisions make it almost impossible for institutional investors to threaten the board in a proxy context. By agreeing to have or adopt a classified board, the institutional investor would be making a gesture of faith in the directors. It would be handing over one instrument that it may later wish to employ to bring pressure to bear.

Super-majority amendments

By similar logic to that used to defend classified board provisions, a super-majority amendment which requires 80 per cent shareholder approval rather than a simple majority of 51 per cent will result in a higher bid for a successful takeover. So a successful bid will surely be better for the institutional investor under a super-majority scenario *provided that a takeover bid is made*. However, the super-majority tactic also increases the likelihood that no such bid will be made and the target firm's shares will continue to sell at a price lower than would be the case under either of the last two options considered. Therefore, the relative advantage of adopting a super-majority amendment is traded off against the risk that such a device will serve only to deter takeover offers and further reduce indirectly the share price.

Anti-takeover mechanisms in general

We have suggested that institutional shareholders should in general oppose anti-takeover mechanisms. However, classified board provisions and super-majority strategies seem to be slightly more acceptable to the institutional investor since they are non-operating defensive measures that require shareholder approval. They have no *direct* effect on the share price paid by potential acquirers and involve no direct wealth transfers to other stakeholders.

There remains the question of how the market will interpret the signal given out by the enactment of an anti-takeover tactic. It may consider that this means that the management of the company in question is overly concerned with protecting its own employment position, in which case the share price will be depressed. Or it may consider that management is behaving in a manner consistent with the long-term interests of the firm, in which case the share price would be expected to rise.

During the 1980s we saw a number of anti-takeover amendments being implemented. At times these devices were used unethically to benefit directors. Mechanisms such as greenmail, golden parachutes and leveraged buyouts were the main culprits in this respect. There is no doubt that some shareholders, stakeholders, communities, and particularly employees have suffered as a result of hostile takeovers.. The rights of some of these groups have been violated. Some commentators have suggested that reforms be instituted to protect these groups from future attempts. This, we believe, would be unhelpful to virtually all concerned.

The evidence regarding anti-takeover tactics is comprehensive and unequivocal:

- According to Greg Jarrell, a member of the Securities and Exchange Commission, of approximately 100 cases studied in which target management defeated a hostile takeover attempt, the defensive tactics resulted almost without exception in large losses of the target shareholders' wealth.

- It has been established that companies which have anti-takeover devices in place do not spend as heavily on research and development as do firms without such devices. In essence anti-takeover devices deprive shareholders of future gains that could be achieved if they were not in place.

It is likely that firms without anti-takeover devices will have larger percentages of institutional investors. Without such devices in place, investors have more power to affect the direction of the company. Institutional investors can become more actively involved in the board's decision-making process and be an active force in the company.

Conclusion

We believe that anti-takeover devices are not in the interests of good corporate governance. Any controls should be enforced, not by the board, but rather by the market in the form of sensible regulations. We reject the notion that takeovers play only a minor role in disciplining managers and that other 'institutions of capitalism' are sufficient to solve the long-documented problem of the separation of ownership and control. The market reacts negatively when mechanisms instituted to discipline managers are circumvented by those same managers.

On the other hand, we certainly agree that boards and senior managers need to get their house in order prior to any potential takeover activity. They need to have asked the question, 'Where might a raider look to improve value?', and to have taken appropriate action based on their answers to benchmark the company against its peer group. And they need to have established an agreed, documented course of action, with all parties identified, against the possibility of an unsolicited bid.

It is sometimes argued that, since shareholders freely choose to vote in favour of anti-takeover amendments then shareholders must take a positive view of such devices. We find this argument unpersuasive. The evidence seem to be that firms passing super-majority amendments, for example, have relatively low institutional shareholdings and relatively high insider holdings. We interpret this as helping to explain how such amendments receive voting approval despite their harmful wealth effects.

Though some anti-takeover devices may benefit some shareholders in specific situations, our recommendation to boards is in general not to contemplate them. Tender offers and hostile takeovers are primary market mechanisms which encourage efficient management and competitive firms. Anti-takeover devices subvert competition in the market for corporate control. 'The refusal of many companies to let raiders buy out their shareholders at a premium flies in the face of one of capitalism's oldest tenets: that a corporation exists to maximise the interests of its shareholders' (Rechner *et al.*).

The debate over anti-takeover devices continues to be played out in the marketplace. In a single month the *Wall Street Journal* reports that over two dozen companies have passed anti-takeover amendments. Most of these companies state that they are unaware of any current, direct takeover threat. At the same time, there is a growing negative shareholder reaction to such measures. As we have said, more and more institutional shareholders are departing from the traditional 'Wall Street Rule' and voting against such proposals in shareholder meetings. In our view, it is incumbent upon boards to promote not just their own interests or those of senior management, but those of their shareholders – and indeed the interests of the business system and society in general.

6 The Control Environment

Confusion

There is some confusion between understanding the importance of the control environment in which an organisation exists and dealing with accounting aspects, which are largely about presentation and form. It is important to distinguish between the two. In our view the more important area to focus on is the control environment because this provides the greatest opportunity to protect value in either commercial or non-profit-making enterprises. In the case of the accounting rules and regulations evidenced in accounting standards and best practice, this demonstrates consistency and clarity of presentation and gives a reasonable chance of understanding the health of that enterprise.

The control environment is concerned with the tone set in the organisation and this starts with the governing body. In the case of a company, the directors and senior management must convey the message and uphold the principle that integrity and effective control cannot be compromised. More formally, the COSO report from which the Cadbury Committee drew so heavily defines the control environment factors to 'include the integrity, ethical values and competence of the entity's people; management's philosophy in operating style; the way management assigns authority and responsibility and organises and develops its people; and the attention and direction provided by the board of directors'.

The controlling body must satisfy itself that there is effective overall control in the organisation that it presides over. This will entail looking beyond the detailed control procedures and ensuring that they are totally comprehensive, cover the identified risks and allow overall control. Understanding of the risks is key to effecting appropriate control.

Background

In a rapidly changing world risks evolve or are created and these need to be managed. The environment in which enterprises or institutions operate may well have significant changes that alter the balance of risks or create significant new ones. For example, businesses, banks, charities and local governments were all impacted by the growth of financial instruments, sometimes esoteric, that had the ability to be used as a hedge against risk or to open up enormous risks that were unrelated to the organisation's main field of endeavour. In consequence, large losses were made by companies and local government, by charities and banking groups, that had neither policy nor controls to limit those risks.

Business enterprises will see risk originate from new competitive activities, from changes in technology and sometimes from regulatory change such as the deregulation of the aircraft industry. This requires a fundamental appraisal by the governing body that sets about identifying the scope of the opportunity, the nature and extent of the risk and what appropriate controls to put in place. Sometimes those latent risks will be geography-based and businesses will need to identify the potential rewards over time, the cost to develop these growing opportunities and the balance of risk to the enterprise itself. A case in point is China with all of the attractions of a large potential domestic market, of a large, cheap labour source, and in some cases indigenous raw materials. A choice needs to be made on what proportion of the assets of the business or perhaps of its development budget should be appropriated there. Future opportunities may be high but there are likely to be setbacks on the path to achievement. Very few companies would be prepared to use China as a sole source for semi-processed or even finished goods production for a worldwide market because the risk in the event of a significant setback, be it political or financial, is just too great.

The same approach is true in a company we spoke with which trades in the former Russian Territories (CIS). Here, the parent company has limited the working capital and the commitments to future production to a level of exposure which the board is comfortable with. While the limit to capital provided and the operational rules are reviewed twice a year, they are set at a level that recognises the potential impact on the business in the event of failure. In other words, if there was a collapse in this area and the working capital was of little or no value, the impact on the group would be manageable.

Governing bodies need to sit down and discuss the areas of greatest risk and the implications that flow from this. Regrettably, there remain a number of businesses and non-profit organisations that have not fully understood the impact of the risks before them. While avoidance of all risks is theoretically possible, it is not desirable in its own right because, inevitably, this approach will have significantly diminished earning opportunities.

Many organisations will sit down to evaluate the greatest risks facing them so that they can formulate appropriate risk-management strategies. There are various levels of risk, as we shall see a little later. First, we need to have a quick look at the broad environment and some views of risk in the community.

Assessing the environment

The operating environment today is one of rapid change when new opportunities and risks appear. A business cannot totally eliminate risk, for this would entail eliminating much of the profit opportunities that go with it. Indeed, classical economic theory will identify profits as being derived from the return for risk. However, thoughtful organisations today are looking for more comprehensive approaches to managing risk. Regrettably, there are controlling bodies that are not fully aware of the risks their organisation faces. As a result, the management of those risks is non-existent or, at best, random. A more rigorous approach to risk management is required if the control environment is to be enhanced. In many enterprises, unfortunately, be they commercial, local government or non-profit, the risks are often complex and not immediately apparent. The task is to identify the major risks, understand the potential impact these might have and put in place an effective process that limits those risks to acceptable proportions.

Some people have a much too narrow view of the risks faced by their organisation. They see them as:

- An insurable risk, perhaps against fire, for loss of profits or non-payment of debtors in a third world country. They may therefore assess the risk carried by the enterprise in relation to the insurance premium.
- Financial risks deriving from treasury policies or using financial derivatives.
- Taking futures contracts for the commodities used in the ordinary course of business.
- The impact of exchange rates on a trans-national company both for translation of profits into the home currency and also the impact on the competitiveness of that company.

These all have dimensions of risk that need to be managed but they do not amount to an adequate understanding of risk. What is needed is a comprehensive view of the risks being faced, an assessment of the probability of the adverse event happening, an evaluation of its likely consequences and a series of steps to control them to acceptable levels.

Sources of risk

Risk can be derived from a wide range of sources which we have summarised in Figure 6.1. We will deal with each of these in turn.

```
• The environment
• Strategic risk
• Asset protection
• Management controls
• Business processes
```

Figure 6.1   Sources of risk

The environment

This is an external threat that may fundamentally change the order of things. In the case of a commercial enterprise there may well be an impact upon the business strategy, perhaps due to changes in the regulation environment or the opening-up of trade previously protected, as we have seen in India for example, or in the airline industry. Other examples could include new competition, new technology or, on a more macro level, a change in government which brings significant changes in approach and impact on different sections of the community. These external forces will materially change the rules of the game, creating significant risk which needs to be evaluated and limits imposed. As a further example, when dealing with new, volatile economies such as China, the board may well decide that there will be some limit to the total assets and new investment in that country, even though this may limit current earnings.

Strategic risk

The preferred strategy of a business should be evaluated not only for its ability to deliver sustainable competitive advantage, but also for its attendant riskiness. The assumptions made will be tested by the governing body so that the degree of risk is understood and accepted. The alternative is for the strategy to be modified. Most boards of directors are aware of the high risk of 'betting the company' on a single action and would shun such an approach to investment decisions.

Asset protection

This is not just a matter for business firms but for much wider enterprises. As an example, charities have sometimes been seduced towards using their inherited assets to produce above average income without recognising the risk to those assets and the implications for the charity. There are plenty of examples in which high-yielding investments in more speculative property or in financial derivatives have caused losses which have destroyed value. Prudence demands a spread of assets, an evaluation of risk through 'what if' analysis and appropriate limits to investment types. Wider implications of asset protection will cover more sophisticated approaches such as hedging borrowings in foreign currencies to match assets or, more appropriately in some cases, to match foreign income streams.

Management controls

By these we mean the processes that are used to assess business risk and the risk controls that are implemented in the organisation. While some organisations try to legislate for all eventualities by means of voluminous manuals, it is perhaps more important to clearly communicate the environment which is desired within the organisation. This will be augmented by creating the appropriate culture using a corporate statement of values that describes the important values held in the ruling body and any operating parts of it. The point is that no manual or set of rules will provide the control environment management wants without all levels of management and the workforce participating with the very essence of values throughout an organisation. Good two-way communication will evoke pride in the enterprise where the reputations of both the organisation itself and its employees are held to be important. This is best achieved through genuine two-way communication so that the 'troops' feel they have participated in agreeing and creating the right control environment. This is quite different from the approach of handing down the laws and rules from the top!

Business controls

Within any organisation the control activities are those policies and procedures that help to ensure management directives are being carried out. These can be preventative, thus ensuring that business processes are operating effectively first time. Alternatively, they can be to detect process failures so that corrective action can be taken. Controls are most effective in an organisation where the culture is one of integrity, high standards and openness in addressing any issues that may arise.

When appropriate business controls are in place they will be supportive of delivering the business objectives and will minimise the risk of unpleasant surprises. Failures should be easier to avoid because earlier thinking will help avoid potential pitfalls. Governing bodies will also have a greater degree of assurance that legal requirements are fully met and that their own ethical standards are being maintained.

However, even the most comprehensive system of controls, checks and balances cannot give the assurance that fraud or failure will be totally eradicated. This is unrealistic, especially where collusion takes place. In a fast-changing world it is also important that the controls and procedures are regularly reviewed to ensure that they remain appropriate to the current environment and the current business challenges.

Businesses operate in a competitive climate so that cost effectiveness is important. This is equally true in the field of business controls where the board will be keen to see that they are designed to balance the cost with the benefits. The benefits should be seen as reduced risk or helping to achieve an improved business performance.

Given the benefits of having an effective control environment and the requirement of the directors to report on the internal control within the company, the board will need to understand the control environment. Many will have such a review undertaken by one of the accounting firms who are widely experienced in this area. Some, usually larger companies, may well have such resource internally that has the skill base and the objectivity to carry out such an approach.

There are many methodologies in helping to focus on the areas of greatest potential impact on the business. We like the hierarchical approach, which is illustrated in Figure 6.2 and which draws on the observations in the COSO report. A review of business controls must be fully supported by management starting from the very top – it is not a task to be left to the internal auditor or the financial accountant.

The best companies pull together into one process the management controls across the different elements of the business. They take the

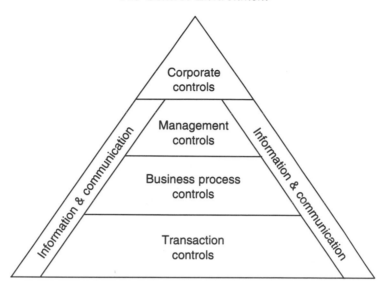

Figure 6.2 What are business controls?

SOURCE: based on the observations of the COSO Report.

different levels of control and look at the impact of potential failure at a high level as well as the lower, more transactional, level.

This approach illustrates that, at the very top level, there is a relatively small number of important corporate controls which the board needs to assess, monitor and review. These then cascade down into management controls, business process controls and finally down to the large number of transaction controls. This contrasts with the old-style approach to controls when a great deal of time was spent verifying in depth a sample of the transaction controls. Today, the much more appropriate and powerful approach is to look at the control environment by assessing the impact of business risks.

It is worth dwelling on this for a moment or two because many business people have a very narrow view of the control process. Within the overall process there are different levels of control which can support the total control framework. Therefore, if the governing body of a company or of a non-profit enterprise wishes to satisfy itself about the effectiveness of overall controls they must first review the total system including the relationships in each part of it.

Turning again to Figure 6.2, we could summarise the position from the top of the triangle as follows:

Level	*Includes*
Corporate controls	• corporate policies
	• control culture and values
	• audit committee
Management controls	• planning and performance monitoring
	• accountabilities
	• risk evaluation
Business process controls	• authorisation
	• validation
	• reconciliation
Transaction controls	• accuracy checks in detail
	• consistency
	• completeness
	• compliance

When such an integrated approach as this is adopted, the governing body will understand, in the fast-changing world in which it operates, what are the key risks the organisation really does face and how well it is prepared to deal with them. We think that internal control can be judged satisfactory if both the governing body (the board of directors in the case of a company) and the executive have reasonable assurance that:

• they understand the extent to which business objectives are being achieved
• published accounts are being prepared reliably
• applicable laws and regulations are being complied with.

Safeway

Safeway, a UK-based plc company with a single business in retail grocery, has an excellent approach to risk assessment.

Breaking the link with the past when lower-level verification was the norm, the internal account function was renamed the 'Business Controls Group'. It developed a new mission which is to add value to the business by 'championing the effective use of business controls'. Uniquely, the Business Controls Group, with its own senior manager, also has a significant input from Coopers & Lybrand which has specialist expertise in this area. This internal audit support is from a separate firm of accountants from the external auditors.

The Business Controls Group believe that to achieve this mission it must concentrate its resource to those areas where it can add most value, which are those areas of greatest risk.

In addition, from the perspective of the business, there is a growing recognition that the ability to demonstrate effective risk management not only brings with it competitive advantage but also contributes to compliance with the Cadbury reporting requirements.

Formalising the risk assessment approach ensures that:

- line management takes accountability for managing risk
- Business Controls focuses its resource on key processes first and gives assurance to the board/audit committee that key risks are being managed effectively
- the comparison of risk between disparate parts of the business is simplified.

In developing the first year's audit plan, Business Controls set itself the goal of having all significant risks within the business identified, assessed and reviewed by the end of the year.

The first stage in the process was to understand the key risks, as identified by the Board of Directors. It is of paramount importance to have the senior managers committed to and contributing to the process of identifying these risks. Business Controls participated in a joint Business Controls/external audit facilitated workshop where the board brainstormed the key risks and performed a top-level prioritisation.

The output from this workshop was taken and the risks assessed in a standard way by the Business Controls Group. By providing a consistent base, the direct comparison of dissimilar risks was permitted and individually prioritised. Once the priority of the risks was known they were divided into two types; those that would benefit from a process review by the Business Controls Group and those that would not.

The process reviews involve the identification and assessment of all risks and controls associated with the process by the people who actually work within that process. This is done using a facilitated workshop which is run by the Business Controls Group but is, most importantly, with the relevant line management. The major activities are to:

- identify, assess and prioritise specific risks of the whole process
- assess control effectiveness
- identify weaknesses and agree control improvements
- establish accountability for implementation and deadlines
- consider all aspects of the integrated control framework

This approach is supported by the close co-ordination that exists with the external auditors as both external audit and Business Controls work to a mutually supportive programme. The whole programme can be seen with its interrelationships in Figure 6.3.

Where Business Controls does not believe that the process review approach will add value, the most appropriate board director is asked to formally consider how that risk is managed. The director is required to 'self certify' that the risk has been reviewed and that it is being controlled appropriately. This certification is passed to Business Controls, which collates responses from all the individual directors and issues a combined report to the board and the audit committee.

This approach has had a number of benefits for the business as well as the Business Controls Group. The business:

- Takes ownership of the controls that manage the risks. Where there is a need for change, management sign on to this as they identified them and they will make them happen.
- Moves away from working in divisional silos. The workshops have representatives from all parts of the process acting as a single team.
- Sees Business Controls Group as an integral and important part of the business. Their facilitation skills mean that they act as catalysts for change, not as policemen.
- Identifies a greater number of risks than through traditional methods – people want to solve problems and this improves the risk management process overall.

There have also been a number of benefits of Business Controls:

- team motivation has significantly increased. They see that they are making a contribution to improving the business, not just criticising it;
- they add value to the business by ensuring a level of cross fertilisation of ideas on controls not seen before in the company. The improved communications they facilitate and the breadth of experience they bring ensures that they are seen as partners, not an overhead;

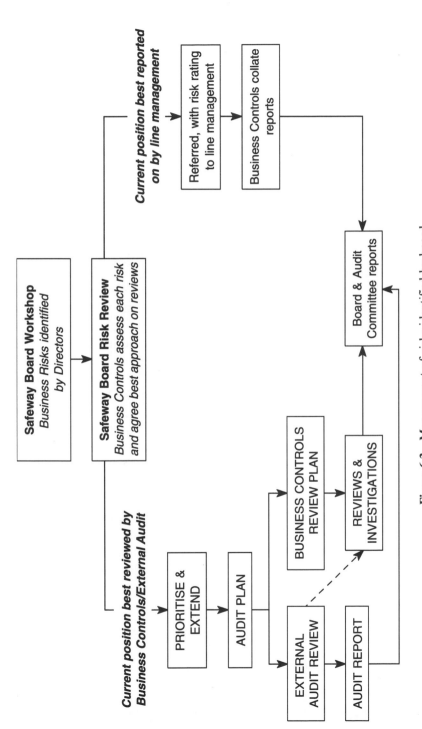

Figure 6.3 Managament of risks identified by board

Reproduced with permission of Safeway Plc.

- reports can be produced more quickly than traditional methods which brings a level of urgency to the improvement process;
- departmental effort and resource goes where it can make a real difference, first time.

All parts of the business are more alert to the key risks that Safeway faces and have a better understanding of the priority for attention. The audit committee is much more effective as it has a clear idea of where the really important risks lie and can monitor actions taken by management to control these.

Universal application

Whatever the organisation – be it the Salvation Army, the local school committee, the village sports club or the mighty corporation – it needs some basic rules that control the actions of its officers. All of these differing bodies have in common the recognition that they are a legal entity, yet, being inanimate, their objectives are achieved through designated officers. In every case real value is added through the provision of standards and rules of conduct that protect the membership as well as other interest groups. These rules are not just financial ones, of course, but will go to the very sense of purpose of the body itself. The setting and maintaining of standards is essential to the maintenance of integrity throughout, which is core. It is for this reason that we have emphasised this element rather than the more presentational aspects of preparing accounting reports according to agreed rules, which themselves are now voluminous, complex and extensive, and in many cases detract from clarity.

The health of the body, be it corporate or non-profit-making, cannot be solely determined by the financial accounts. There are indeed non-accounting measures that will help to give a more balanced view. To get a flavour of some of these let us look at some relevant non-accounting measures for a non-profit-making body. Depending upon its purpose these could include:

- Net membership gains or losses
- External assessment of effectiveness (of a charity)
- Public awareness (prompted and unprompted)
- Recognition – trophies won
- Governing body's assessment of the degree to which objectives were achieved to time.

Small and non-profit organisations

There will be other specific items that apply in certain circumstances which are worth the trouble identifying by those controlling such bodies. The question to ask is 'What key measures best describe our performance?' External assessment is often helpful to the ruling body of, say, the charity or sports club both to avoid self deception and perhaps to use as evidence for fundraising. In the United Kingdom, the charity Co-operation Ireland will conduct such external research that gives a sound foundation for future activities as well as providing good data to enhance its fundraising.

However, this chapter is mainly focused on financial aspects. In common with the great worldwide companies, smaller companies or non-profit organisations need to have financial rules and controls as an important part of maintaining their health. There are some principles that can be applied almost universally:

- Proper books of accounts must be kept up to date at all times and properly reconciled with appropriate physical assets or liabilities.
- Accounts should be regularly drawn up to an appropriate time schedule and be reconciled back to the books of account.
- Appropriate supporting information should be properly filed and available when required.
- An agreed form of authority for expenditure should be documented and practised.
- A clear record of decisions of the appropriate seat of governance.
- A segregation of duties of officers that enables checks and balances in the structure and a clear limit of authorities.
- The governing body has a clear understanding of the areas of major risk and how this risk is managed.
- In almost every case the organisation's books and accounts should be audited by a suitably qualified and independent auditor.

There must be an opportunity for the ruling body to examine the statement of accounts prior to approving these. Here, members will be concerned to satisfy themselves that the accounts present a true and fair picture of the activities for the period under review. In drawing this conclusion they will ask questions such as:

- Broadly do the accounts show that we were close to our plan and expectations? If not, can we satisfactorily explain the differences?

- Are we satisfied that where judgements are required, perhaps for example on the value of investments or debtors, that these are valid and consistent?
- Are there any omissions, say, for unrecorded liabilities or assets not reflected in the accounts?

It is a great benefit to have the auditor report in person to the full governing body so that members can question him or her on the extent of the audit and qualitative issues that may have arisen. It also gives an opportunity to learn more about the control environment and any areas of significant weaknesses. This personal contact is indeed a very important part of the task of an audit committee in larger public companies.

The corporate sector

Throughout this book there are references to gaps between the expectations of the community at large and the ability to deliver these. This applies to boards of directors as we have seen in Chapter 2. It certainly applies as well to audit committees and, for different reasons, the remuneration committee is also highly unlikely to satisfy the widely different demands of sectional interests. A question often asked is whether a good system of governance or even more rules and legislation in a company, is likely to prevent company failures. The regrettable answer is no; but there is every expectation that a climate of good governance would make widespread fraud or financial failure less likely.

Let us for a moment dwell on the causes of company failures. Coopers & Lybrand's experience was included in their June 1992 briefing following the Cadbury Report. They especially emphasised that 'dominant executive directors (are) not living up to their duties as stewards of a public company; overambition; failure to take advice from non-executives (or their failure to give it); and failure to follow basic controls'. Coopers & Lybrand believe that an environment which allows this to happen 'inevitably also facilitates dishonesty'. A summary of the experience of this accounting firm which has a large audit as well as insolvency practice shows the causes of failure listed in Figure 6.4. We would add to this list, insufficient attention to cash flow through an over-reliance on the earnings per share which are often used to trigger executive bonus schemes.

1. *Board control*
   - overdominant CEO or executive team
   - inadequate or biased information to the board
   - unbalanced boards in terms of skills
   - strategies based on short term share price rather than solid, real earnings
   - inadequate systems of financial control

2. *Financial exposure*
   - overly complex dealings exploiting inconsistencies in regulatory regimes
   - overly complex financing
   - failure to change policies with changing economic conditions
   - insufficient control of financial transactions or failure to evaluate risks with these

3. *Expansion*
   - lack of realism in take-overs and over paying
   - inability to manager overseas investments
   - insufficient managerial resource

4. *Response to problems*
   - unwillingness to admit failure or bad news

Figure 6.4 Recent causes of company failures

Audit committee

Within the corporate sector the role of the audit committee is pivotal in at least helping to provide checks and balances and pressure to raise standards of consistent, clear, factual reporting. However, as we will see later in this chapter, the expectations of the community are varied but in many respects incapable of being fully satisfied. Despite this, audit committees are very important and increasingly relied upon and used. Ernst & Young note in their *New Directions for Audit Committees* that a recent survey of finance directors indicated what they would most like to see in corporate governance. Top of the list by far (more than 25 per cent of respondents) was agreement with the comment that 'increased power of non-executive directors and audit committees is fundamental in protecting shareholders from malpractice at board level'.

History

Audit committees are not new although they are largely Anglo-Saxon. In Australia and Canada, all listed companies are required by law to have audit committees. Other countries such as USA and UK make this a listing requirement of the Stock Exchange. It is interesting to trace the evolution of the audit committee within the corporate board structure. The need to prevent fraud, cognitive omissions and management error were the prime reasons for their creation.

As an example, in USA following the 1940 McKesson–Robbins fraud, the Securities and Exchange Commission (SEC) recommended that audit committees be formed to afford 'the greatest possible protection to investors and shareholders alike'.

This was reaffirmed in 1972 by the SEC with the additional recommendation that the committees be comprised of non-executive directors. In 1974, the SEC required a publicly listed company to disclose in the annual report whether or not it had an audit committee and, if so, its membership. The committee's only prescribed role at this time was to appoint the auditor and negotiate the audit agreement. This was followed by the guidelines developed in 1987 by the Treadway Commission which was formed from a number of accounting bodies. These recommendations are summarised in Figure 6.5.

Following the 1965 collapse of the Atlantic Acceptance Corporation Limited, the Canadian Government established a Royal Commission which recommended that an audit committee should examine the financial statements before they were presented to the full board. Since then, fairly standard additional requirements have been made which we have reflected along with others in Figure 6.6.

In the United Kingdom, the history is not dissimilar but the most significant landmark is 1992 when the Cadbury Committee reported on Financial Aspects of Corporate Governance. External auditors must comment on the company's compliance with Cadbury in their annual report. A key recommendation is that all listed companies should have an audit committee and they provide specimen terms of reference which are helpful. All of these suggestions together form a fairly formidable, even unmanageable, list which is highlighted in Figure 6.5.

If we were to combine Figures 6.5 and 6.6, a very long list of potential activities for the audit committee would be produced. The reader will readily see, given both the long list, and the experience and time available of non-executive directors who are members of the audit committee, that this prescribed approach is difficult.

- All public companies should develop a written charter (terms of reference) setting forth the duties and responsibilities of the audit committee. The board of directors should approve the charter, review it periodically, and modify it as necessary.

- Audit committees should be informed, vigilant, and effective overseers of the financial reporting process and the company's internal controls.

- The audit committee should review annually the programme that management establishes to monitor compliance with the code of conduct.

- Management and the audit committee should ensure that the internal auditor's involvement in the audit of the entire financial reporting process is appropriate and properly co-ordinated with the independent public accountant.

- Audit committees should have adequate resources and authority to discharge their responsibilities, including the discretion to initiate investigation and to engage outside experts.

- The audit committee should review management's evaluation of factors relating to the independence of the company's public accountant. Both the audit committee and management should assist the public accountant in preserving his or her independence.

- Before the beginning of each year, the audit committee should review management's plans for engaging the company's public accountant to perform management advisory services during the coming year, considering both the types of services that may be rendered and the projected fees.

- Management should advise the audit committee when it seeks a second opinion on a significant accounting issue.

- The annual report should contain a letter outlining the responsibilities and activities of the audit committee during the year.

- The audit committee should comprise non-executive directors.

- Audit committees should oversee the quarterly reporting process.

Figure 6.5 Treadway Commission's recommendations for audit committees, 1987

It is, in our view, not the most productive pathway. The basic assumption made in the early formation of audit committees –that they would have the ability to prevent fraud – is a mistaken one. On average, an audit committee may meet between 8 to 10 hours a year. Even with the most appropriate agenda and diligent, qualified members, it would not be able to make such a claim. It is, of course, worth remembering that external auditors would not be able to give such an undertaking even after a rigorous audit.

- Audit committees for large institutions (assets of US$ 3 billion) are required to include two members with financial experience, have the specific ability to engage their own legal counsel, and must not include any large customers of the institution.

- Audit committee to examine and approve the financial statements prior to submission to the full board.

- Audit committees should review the interim results as well as the annual results.

- Consist of no fewer than three persons.

- Meet in executive session with internal auditing, senior management and the independent accountant.

- Periodically report the results of its reviews to the full board.

- If there is a change in the independent accountant, the audit committee should review all issues related to the change and review all reportable events, disagreements and unresolved issues on a timely basis.

- Review the audit plan of the independent accountant.

- Review any proposed changes in significant accounting policies, significant risks and uncertainties and key estimates and judgements.

- Discuss all significant issues raised during the audit.

- Obtain from management an explanation of significant variances between periods.

- Review the management letter received from the internal auditor and the independent accountant and their activity to follow up any identified weaknesses.

- Review all public disclosure documents containing audited or unaudited financial information prior to release.

- Review the terms of reference of the internal auditing group.

- Review the appointments of the CFO and other key financial executives.

- Review transactions and investments that could adversely affect the well-being of the institution or the auditors and the actuaries.

- Should usually meet twice a year.

- CFO and internal auditor should attend meetings.

- Audit committee should meet with auditor once a year without management present.

- Should have access to any information and be able to use outside experts as needed.

Figure 6.6 Recommendations from various enquiries and commissions, additional to Treadway

New direction

Given the differing expectations from different parts of the community which in total cannot be met, is there a question about the audit committee's value? In practice, is the audit committee nothing more than a fancy decoration of the company to show in a glitzy way that governance is at work? We think not. We believe that audit committees will become more important and more influential in raising standards.

An effective audit committee should be capable of providing the following benefits:

1. Support and reinforcing within the company a culture of openness in reporting and of high ethical standards of conduct in fiscal matters.
2. Creating an environment within the company of consciousness of controls and of risks and of managing these risks to agreed limits.
3. Helping to reduce the risk of financial loss from fraud and other illegal or improper acts.
4. Providing objectivity on financial judgements to be made in the accounts, especially on those occasions when there may be a disagreement between management and auditors. Often the audit committee will be an effective sounding board for any issues of concern for the finance director.
5. Reinforcing the independence of auditors and of any internal audit function.
6. Improving the quality of financial reporting and the consistency of those accounts. This will include discussions on accounting policy, financial reporting standards and the presentation of external reports.

In our experience, many audit committees do not achieve the impact that they are capable of because they focus on the easier, mechanistic aspects of their role. They review the accounts, they are led through the proposed audit programme and 'sign off' on the audit fee agreed by the management. The area that is less well addressed is assessing the control environment by understanding the real nature of the risks the company faces, how these might impact and how they are being managed. What are the areas of greatest risk that the business is exposed to and what would be the financial impact? As a practical suggestion, the audit committee chairman can arrange quality agenda time for executive directors to appear before the audit committee and explain exactly how they control their part of the business. It is often insightful to see if the extent and implications of the risks facing the business are clearly identified. The next step is to demonstrate the controls that are in place and the weight given to this aspect of management, then to test how the executive *knows* it is controlled.

Practical example

The evolution of an audit committee as it strives to first be recognised, second to start to add value and then to have a significant impact often follows the pattern mentioned above. This can also be seen in Case Study 6.1, where Jack Jones reflects on the seven years since he was appointed chairman of the audit committee from its inception. The focus on the control environment is a very important area for audit committees in the future.

── Case Study ──

Evolution of an audit committee

During our discussions on financial aspects of corporate govern-ance we spoke with a senior partner of one of the big six accounting firms who shared with us his experience with one of his audit clients, a FTSE 100 company. We were also able to have a follow-up discussion with the Chairman of the Audit Committee. The company, which we will call Progressive Holdings Plc, formed an audit committee in 1988. It was headed up by a newly recruited, non-executive director who had been a chief executive of an international manufacturing company until he retired early some six months prior to joining Progressive's board. We will call him Jack Jones.

Jones had been a finance director many years back and had a good understanding of accounting principles but did not consider himself especially knowledgeable on accounting standards or the latest accounting thinking. However, he believed that the audit committee was an important element in lifting standards of governance at Progressive. The committee consisted of himself and two other non-executive directors together with the company secretary who undertook the staff work. The chief executive and the finance director attended each meeting. The first task was to set out the purpose of the committee, showing how it related to the board and the broad areas it covered.

As Jack Jones says, 'In those early years we were trying to comply with the London Stock Exchange request for all major issues of audit and control to be referred to the newly formed audit committee. The initial focus was on the annual accounts where the committee would spend time trying to understand the issues and judgements in more depth than would have been possible in a regular board meeting. There was also a short meeting at the half year where we may also look at a special topic such as the treasury report before it was submitted to the board.' The early agendas consisted of items drawn from the following headings:

- reviewing the statutory accounts;
- understanding the judgements made in arriving at the end results;
- clarifying with the auditors any items of concern;
- reviewing the major audit issues, if any, which may have been of significance to the company;
- approval of audit fees negotiated by the executive management;
- a few ad hoc items such as treasury report, funding plans or a more detailed review of a very large item of capital expenditure.

Jones reflects that 'In the early years we were struggling to make a really meaningful contribution. We were poorly prepared as, in truth, no one undertook any special training but rather relied on advice from the auditors and then they used their best collective judgements on the agenda items. Naturally enough, I tried to read as much as possible to improve my knowledge base.'

Both the auditors and Jones believed that the committee was a helpful step forward and they were clear that the audit committee added value. At this time the debate about the merits of audit committees was in full swing.

When the Cadbury recommendations were made, the Progressive board were pleased to observe that they complied almost completely with the recommendations. However, they felt that, from the viewpoint of both improving the control environment and reducing the external audit fees, an internal audit department should be set up. The newly appointed internal auditor reported directly to the Group Finance Director but with a strong relationship to the Chair of the Audit Committee. The internal auditor was then appointed Secretary to the Audit Committee in place of the Company Secretary.

Jack Jones felt that this was a significant step forward as the internal auditor would agree audit committee agendas with him and this would give him greater control of the environment. Certainly, there was a greater knowledge of the group through the information provided by the internal audit department. It was also felt that there was a greater knowledge of internal control within the group and a more comprehensive understanding of audit issues. There were then new dimensions of the audit committee which included:

- the planned approach to audit including the integration of the internal and external audits
- a review of significant areas of concern from the 'health check' internal audits of individual operations in different parts of the world
- reviewing accounting standards and their implications for Progressive Holdings Plc.

Jack Jones felt that for the first time he was, as Chair, better informed about the group and that he had more control over the appropriate agenda for the committee. Further, he felt that he had the appropriate resource to undertake his duties professionally.

As a separate appraisal process over the effectiveness of the audit committee, the Chair talked to his fellow non-executive members and the auditors. There was general agreement that this audit committee was functioning well. The auditors assessed the committee's effectiveness under three main headings in order to make their observations on effectiveness.

1. Understanding , assessing and monitoring the control environment.
2. Promoting sound financial reporting.
3. Upholding standards of business conduct.

However, the individual non-executives were discomforted in a number of areas. First, they felt they had insufficient technical knowledge to be really sure about the degree to which the financial reporting was sound. Second, they felt inadequately informed over the business risks to make real judgements about the control environment.

Jack Jones responded by ensuring that all members of the committee received accounting publications on standards, the future direction of audit committees and special reports such as Greenbury. He also increased audit committee meetings to not less than three or more than four per annum with the agenda covering items that would improve the level of understanding of committee members. This included greater understanding of the business risk, how this is managed and what the main controls are. Other items would include a review of internal audit activities and especially a review of a particular business within the group where this is troublesome or large in the group context.

In the future, Jack Jones wants to see in place procedures across the group that will enable Progressive to make public statements about the state of internal control with sufficient quality work to enable this to be audited. He believes that there is much more work needed on understanding in depth the nature and extent of business risks being faced in Progressive Holdings and how these are being managed within the company. While he feels good about the progress during the period of his stewardship, he knows that members of the audit committee must continue to improve their knowledge base given the rapid changes taking place in accounting, corporate governance and the business environment in total.

The company chairman has a decision to make because Jack Jones has completed two three-year terms as a non-executive and is on a year-by-year tenure. Although he is only 63 years of age, the company needs to rotate its non-executive directors to comply with Cadbury. Jones's replacement will almost certainly need to be an external one!

Internal control

Universally important

While the internal control of a business will be a key item on the audit committee's agenda, it deserves separate attention because of its importance. Further, any business or indeed any non-profit organisation needs to be satisfied that the internal control system is satisfactory and is operating in practice. An internal control system usually consists of documented procedures, often formally embodied in an accounting manual, and lists the checks required of management to ensure the sanctity of the control environment. This will help to ensure that the assets of the business are safeguarded and that the liabilities are properly incurred, recorded and managed. The records will of course need to be accurate, easy to follow and fully reflect reality! Regrettably, we have seen occasions when the books of account were perfectly kept within the rules laid down but were fictitious in that they did not reconcile back to the actual assets and liabilities.

When the internal control environment is examined, it is helpful also to review the attitude to control procedures from the top of the organisation to the very 'coal face'. This is at least equal in importance to verifying the facts because it will show the climate of the organisation in its real force. Good control procedures and a climate that is very supportive of control are key elements of good governance and key to ensuring that the accounts produced are reliable.

Recommended by Cadbury

The Cadbury Committee also recognised this as an important area. They recommend as part of the code of best practice for listed companies 'that the directors should make a statement in the report and accounts on the affectiveness of their system of internal control and that the auditors should report thereon'.

The problem is that there is not as yet a standard basis for undertaking this task and certainly a number of audit firms are declining to comment on the statement. Part of the reason for this is the potential for liability if subsequently internal controls were seen to be ineffective in a particular area, resulting in law suits! This topic is still being discussed by the accounting and audit bodies. Some companies, such as B.P. and Redland, have reviewed the state of internal control within the company but make no judgement about how effective these controls are in practice. Meanwhile, pioneers like Guinness and Coats Viyella have elected to review the effectiveness of internal control, giving an opinion on its effectiveness, and certainly Deloitte Touche are now prepared to offer an opinion on the statement. Perhaps as more audit firms turn themselves into limited liability companies they will not feel so nervous in offering an opinion!

The board

The board, or its audit committee or the controlling body in a non-profit organisation, must have some firm basis for satisfying itself that proper controls are in place. They will:

- Ensure that accounting procedures are clearly in place.
- Understand the major risks in the business and how these are controlled.
- Watch for any trends of weakening of control from internal audit reports, the external auditor and general observation on the climate of control.
- Ensure that there is an appropriate segregation of duties.
- Understand and test the pathway by which the conclusion on the state of internal control has been reached.

Dealing with this last point will require a specific process that flows from the bottom of the company to the top which will give sufficient confidence on any conclusion reached. To achieve this it is helpful to have one common check list. Such an approach is illustrated in Neville Bain's book *Successful Management* (Figure 10.1) which is reproduced here in Figure 6.7.

However, there is another aspect of the role of the board that has important implications for the future viability and value of the corporation that needs to be addressed. This is the question of the board's approach to strategic financing sisues. While, given its centrality, this is a topic that has been addressed in the chapter on the role of the board, it is important to highlight some aspects here, given that there are strong implications for company control.

Many board agendas which we have seen have a relatively heavy emphasis on reviewing history or making ad hoc decisions on investments, especially capital expenditure. In many cases the corporate finance type of decisions which have a significant long-term effect are often not fully assessed for the strategic or longer-term impact on the enterprise. The record is better in the better-run companies where an assessment is usually made of the change to the risk profile of the business. However, the board needs to be more proactive in assessing the risk and longer-term implications in the following areas:

THE COMPANY Plc

Accounting Controls Checklist

Statement by the Managing and Finance Directors of:

Unit/company..........................

At the year end and subject to the exceptions explained in a separate commentary:

1. The Management Returns (MRs) for the year end were prepared on the basis of a fully extracted and extended trial balance from the general ledger, including appropriate provision for accruals and prepayments, and comprehensive cut-off procedures.
2. A full stocktake was performed at year end and the valuation thereof was reconciled to both the detailed stock records and/or the book (financial) stock. Significant variances were fully investigated and appropriate adjustments made.
3. Adequate but not excessive provision was made for stock obsolescence on a reliable and systematic basis, consistent with that adopted at the year end.
4. Adequate but not excessive provision was made for bad and doubtful debts on a reliable and systematic basis, consistent with that adopted at the year end.
5. All inter-company balances were fully reconciled with corresponding company units balances, differences fully investigated and appropriate adjustments made.
6. All key control accounts were fully reconciled and appropriate adjustments made.
7. All suspense accounts were fully analysed/reconciled and appropriate adjustments made.

Managing Director ....   Signed: ....

Financial Director ....   Signed: ....

Dated: ....

Figure 6.7 Accounting controls checklist

1. Funding policy and plans, e.g.
   - hedging policy
   - use of derivatives
   - fixed and floating rates
   - committed facilities
2. Treasury policy
   - managing tax effective flows to the home base
3. Taxation review
   - international tax management with risks and opportunities spelt out
   - transfer pricing
   - compliance
   - disputes

These are very different from accounting presentation issues or compliance with the various codes. Regrettably, in too many cases, boards of directors have not addressed these issues formally.

Board actions

Just as the board of directors of the great majority of public companies allocate time to understand and test the strategy of the business, so too should they allocate the time that is needed to ensure that the control environment is effective. In a number of cases the board may well delegate this task to the audit committee which should have the time and the competence to undertake this task. There may well be a case for professional help to ensure thoroughness and objectivity. Where the audit committee undertakes this task they must report back to the full board as all directors are responsible to ensure that the controls are appropriate and satisfactory. While it will be obvious that every organisation, whether commercial or not-for-profit, has a need for effective control, the approach will vary depending upon the size.

The review process which should be updated on a regular, perhaps annual, basis will require the board to:

- consider if it has clearly set out and communicated its policies on key risk items, on ethical standards and values
- determine whether it is satisfied that there is a dependable process in place that provides assurance to the board on the effectiveness of controls

- undertake a review and update of the schedule of matters reserved for board decisions
- as a regular exercise, have key executive directors and other senior executives talk to the board or the audit committee about the key risks that their business faces and how they have gone about controlling these
- determine if they are satisfied with the process of evaluation and review of internal control effectiveness, thus enabling them to annually make the statement required under the Cadbury Code of Practice
- consider if sufficient time and exposure has been given to any areas that are know to be weaker in control or where change is rapidly talking place
- ensure that responsibilities for controls are clearly identified and allocated specifically

These are positive steps that can be taken which will improve the control environment. A very comprehensive approach to identifying key business and financial risks is included in appendix 4 of Coopers & Lybrand's publication *Effective Business Controls: a Guide for Directors* which was published in 1993. They have provided a detailed set of questions which directors may wish to use. We have reproduced this in Figure 6.8 with the permission of the authors.

Summary

There is value in having high standards of internal control and, more widely, in placing weight behind financial aspects of governance. This requires a clear understanding of the risks faced by the business and how these are managed. While there remain plenty of organisations that are paying lip-service to this, our evidence suggests that more and more see this as a fruitful area to add value. Certainly, the reputation of the organisation is enhanced, with all of the positive benefits this brings. During our discussions we found a group of business people who felt that the focus on financial aspects of corporate governance was a bit of a chore but that it would at least limit any damages if a future court action was launched. This may be a valid, minority view but it certainly demeans the whole area of governance and limits the benefits from applying resource to it.

Figure 6.8

Questions directors may wish to address in identifying key business and
financial risks include the following:

Board and organisational structure

Is the operation of the board open and frank or is there a risk that senior
executives could be playing down some issues of real concern?
Does the board have a clear strategy for the group?
Does the whole board receive sufficient information to be aware of business
and financial risks on a timely basis?
Does financial information coming to the board appear to be reliable?
Does the board have sufficient information from operating subsidiaries,
especially overseas?
Is the board removed from the business?
Do senior executives appear competent for their duties?

Accountability

Does the board understand and accept its responsibilities towards the investing
public?
Are there areas, such as executive terms of employment, where shareholders
might feel they have cause to complain?

Control environment

Has the board adequately communicated its policies on key risks and its
attitude to control failure or illegal or unethical behaviour?
Are there lessons to be learned from past control failures in relation to both
specific risks and general attitudes within the organisation to control?
Are mechanisms for monitoring the quality of controls adequate?
Are executives facing unrealistically demanding budgets or bonus schemes that
could create incentives to cut corners or misreport results?
Do incentive schemes encourage management to ensure effective compliance
and control?
Do personnel policies limit the risk of employing dishonest or insufficiently
competent staff?
Are IT strategies and resources consistent with the business objectives?
Where might the group be exposed to loss through fraud or negligence?
If a director or senior manager were so minded, how easy would it be for him
or her to defraud the group?
Are authority levels of senior executives clearly agreed?
Do significant transactions and commitments require specified high level
authorisations?

Figure 6.8 continued overleaf

Figure 6.8 continued

Group assets

Does the group have substantial assets that are susceptible to theft, deterioration, wide fluctuations in value or obsolescence?
Are highly liquid assets properly safeguarded including separation of responsibilities in relation to handling the assets and authorising transactions?
Might group assets be applied to non-group purposes?
Are there particular physical dangers associated with group operations?
Are there adequate disaster recovery plans?

Products, services and markets

Are the group's markets facing particularly difficult conditions, eg from changes in customer demand or levels of competition?
Is the group heavily reliant on a small number of customers or types of customers?
Are there substantial risks of being sued by customers, employees or others, eg for product liability?
What are the risks associated with faulty goods or services or with goods being tampered with after they leave the group's control?
Is there a risk of infringing patent rights?
Does the supply of raw materials, skilled labour or capital equipment pose difficulties?
Are there risks associated with the way the group promotes and markets its goods or services?
Where the group uses agents, sub-contractors or representatives, do they pose a financial or reputational threat to the group?

Regulatory environment

Are there regulations (including taxation) to which the business is subject where failure could lead to serious difficulties for the business, eg through fines, loss of reputation or loss of licences?
Is the group in a fiduciary position in relation to other parties (eg as investment manager)?
Are there significant environmental concerns?
Are there major litigation problems?

Change

Is there rapid or substantial change or uncertainty in the business or its environment?
Is there new legislation expected which will have a major impact on the business?
Is the business keeping pace with technological change?
Are acquisitions properly controlled?

Figure 6.8 continued overleaf

Figure 6.8 continued

Financial risks

Is the group highly geared or heavily reliant on short-term sources of finance?
Is there a risk that the company might be in breach of loan covenants or borrowing limits?
Is the group financially exposed, eg to interest rate or currency fluctuations?
How effective are banking relationships?
Are there major commitments or contingent liabilities?
Does the group have highly complex financial dealings?
Is cost and other management information reliable as a basis for strategic business decisions?
Is cash forecasting effective?
Does the group have any unusual or aggressive accounting policies or any figures in internal or external account which are highly subjective?
Does the group have significant loss-making activities?
Is there any question over the going concern status of the business?
Is the finance function adequately qualified and resourced?
Are control account reconciliations and balances reviewed?
Are cheque payments adequately documented and authorised?
Are receipts securely handled and promptly banked?
Are computer systems and files properly protected from interference?

Figure 6.8   Identifying key business and financial risks

SOURCE: Reproduced from Cooper & Lybrand, *Effective Business Control: a Guide for Directors* (1993) (with permission).

However, we are heartened by the growing number of organisations that are putting the time and effort into this field to make genuine advances for the benefits of the organisation. There is, though, a strong plea from almost all sections of the community we spoke with. Allow business a couple of years to improve the position without more directives or legislation. 'The practice is what needs to improve. This will not be the case if more and more legislation comes through.' People are increasingly fearful of European legislation and, given the bureaucratic, non-accountable nature of Brussels, we can understand that concern.

7   Governance of Not-for-Profit Enterprises

Introduction

This chapter investigates the notion of corporate governance as far as the board of a non-profit enterprise is concerned. We shall discuss various recurring issues confronting Boards of Directors. We shall look especially at the distinction between direction and management as it relates to organisations in this sector. We are concerned to suggest ways in which the relationship between Directors and managers can be made as non-competitive as possible.

How is the not-for-profit sector different?

The most familiar tension within a not-for-profit organisation is between a director, often with an exclusively commercial background, wishing the organisation to be put on a more commercial footing, and employees objecting to what they see as the director's attempt to turn the organisation into a commercial enterprise. But perhaps the next most familiar tension is over precisely these same questions within the employees themselves.

For some not-for-profit entities, however, the argument has long ago been resolved. They have taken the view that the prime requirement for their sustainability is to operate in the most resource-effective way they can. Typically, this requires them to adopt genuinely *business* practices. This they have done with greater or lesser degrees of enthusiasm. There is little doubt that this has been the pattern in recent years. There have been a number of reasons for this trend.

First, the not-for-profit sector has not been immune from fluctuations in the broad macroeconomic environment. Whenever those fluctuations have been negative, it has been incumbent on organisations in all sectors to behave in a more efficient manner. Second, in such a climate, large-scale benefactors of the sector, particularly the government, have increasingly demanded (and travelled down) transparent audit trails, in order to be satisfied about the management of their contributions.

Third, there has been a growing tendency for not-for-profits to hire their executives from the private sector. Fourth, and in the light of the first development, the ongoing downsizing trend in the private sector has provided not-for-profits with a sizeable bank of potential managers. Fifth, many longer-serving not-for-profit employees have themselves come to value the potential added value to their operations of contemporary business techniques.

Sixth, one of the manifestations of this last trend has been that many such employees have taken up post-graduate or post-experience business studies. Finally, many higher education providers have in turn offered a number of programmes aimed specifically at this sector. Unsurprisingly, these various developments have affected the management styles of not-for-profits. This is particularly the case for those organisations which in the past have not been particularly focused on either transparency of responsibilities or performance audit.

It is even truer of organisations which have actively discouraged the involvement of employees in strategic planning activities. Now it is much more likely that such staff will have to engage in disciplined planning processes and to take clear accountability for discrete elements of the organisation's operations. It is equally likely that they will be part of a systematic process of appraisal against agreed targets. Such a cultural metamorphosis must have posed major difficulties for many long-serving members of not-for-profit organisations.

On the other hand, it is observably true that these changes have also brought about a general enhancement of operational effectiveness and marketing practice in not-for-profits. What they have not generally brought about, however, has been a closer working relationship between executives and directors. As funders and clients of the sector have become more demanding, and as managers within the sector have become more conversant with modern management disciplines, so have the hopes vested in the directors grown.

The greater importance attached to directors' potential for furthering the association's goals has met with varying dividends as far as their actual performance has been concerned. Reasons for this include the problem – generic to all boards and discussed elsewhere in this book – of the available days per annum to devote to these duties; frequent changes of director personnel and the absence of appropriate developmental programmes for such directors. The outcome has often been serious tensions between management and board. The executive arm of the organisation can react to this by maintaining its distance from the directors. Frequent manifestations of this are senior managers orchestrating directors' agendas and meetings, provision of less then complete data to the board, and a pose of condescension by managers to directors.

Many not-for-profit employees are apparently concerned that, when presented with the chance, directors will interfere with the executive processes of the organisation. There is no doubt that there is considerable evidence of this occurring. There are many examples of not-for-profit directors, with significant commercial backgrounds, effectively becoming 'executives at one remove'. Often this has happened while employees with little talent for management have stepped back and allowed it to happen. Thus both sides have contributed to a mischievous confusion of responsibilities. Directors have a duty to direct and moderate. It is not their responsibility to *administer*. It is relatively unimportant if a director has no particular knowledge of the sector or detailed awareness of the workings of the association on whose board he or she sits. Such a director may still carry out a critical stewardship role so long as the right organisational architecture is in place and routine administration is not seen as part of a director's brief. Too many not-for-profit organisations blur responsibilities for information exchange and this erodes executives' proper spheres of influence

The extent of the problem

The other effect of such a blurring is the potentially more critical one of weakening the association's fundamental connection with its benefactors and clients. This negative outcome can be achieved as well if too free a rein is given to a lingering mistrust in the sector of anything imported from 'industry'. It is fairly easy to detect those organisations where such distrust remains prevalent. They are those which have inflicted nomenclature torture on themselves. Their boards are 'governing bodies' or 'councils'. Their managers are administrators or organisers. The 'B' and 'M' words are to be avoided at all costs. This, of course, further increases the potential for muddiness and inconsistency. If an organisation is determined not to use the 'B' word, then it may well lose sight of some of the fundamental characteristics of a board's true role. The outcome can only be a less useful organisation for the clients it exists to serve. Indeed, one of the more disturbing sights in this sector has been the number of boards which have been struggling, over a long period, to find a method and a function not at odds with their associations' configuration and philosophy.

Regrettably for their clients, some organisations have waged this struggle in vain. There are, we believe, some structural impediments in the not-for-profit sphere which have slowed directors' attempts to articulate their brief. An inconsistent and unsettled political and bureaucratic environment, relatively dormant patrons, and dynamic financial circumstances have all had their effects. Some organisations have opted for 'the science of muddling through', and have regarded each year survived in such a fashion as an achievement. Others have just not been able to find the time to devote to the construction of considered methods and architectures, despite their acknowledgment that the existing systems are insufficient for this new environment. The net result is that no clear blueprint for board practice in this sector has emerged. In addition, the 'anti-industry' bias; the discretionary nature of the sector; the ambiguity over an association's *raison d'être*; the misapprehension of the differences between an executive and a directional role; and membership difficulties have all delayed the emergence of such a blueprint.

One serious outcome of this has been that directors in this sector have too rarely 'gone to school' on their commercial equivalents. This has led to their continuing with long-outmoded customs. The worst of these is the failure to understand the distinction between the directional and executive roles, and the differing duties of employees and directors. A fundamental requirement for all voluntary associations, we believe, is for them to understand that employees' duty of administration needs to be quite distinct from the board's duty of direction.

Explaining the board/executive muddle

Elsewhere in this book, we elaborate on the differences between directing and managing, and we shall not rehearse them here. What is important here is to acknowledge that *doing* something about those differences is not always without difficulty. In the not-for-profit sector, a large number of directors are chosen precisely because of their business skills and knowledge appropriate to the association's sphere of interest. In some cases, they are selected by an external body, in other cases they are chosen by ballot. Irrespective of their mode of entry on to the board, however, they must comprehend and put into practice the fact that their responsibility is not to administer but to direct.

Necessarily, this will involve avoiding the numerous chances that will present themselves to become involved in the organisation's internal processes. A failure to carry out such a self-denying ordinance will lead to tension between employees and directors. The outcome will be a less vigorous performance on behalf of clients. It can be a great temptation for a director with the kind of background described above to want to import the latest management practices to the organisation, or to give it the benefit of his or her years of management experience. In our view, either desire is wrong-headed. A director who is tempted in this way should stick to their board role, and keep off of the executives' patch. But how is this to be done?

It is essential that directors devolve complete accountability for all executive areas to the highest-ranking executive. This is a zero-sum matter. Directors often struggle with this black and white requirement. Voluntary associations, in general, do not have a brilliant operational history. As we have seen, this is partly due to a bias against 'industry' and all its works. It is due as well to directors taking a condescending view of relatively amateurish but amiable employees. The result has been a preparedness to put up with low levels of executive performance. In such circumstances, a vicious circle spins into action, and directors with a commercial management background are understandably not attracted by the notion of devolving management responsibilities. Worse, however, are those circumstances in which directors continue to involve themselves in the executive sphere, despite the executives being highly competent and despite a general preparedness on directors' parts to devolve responsibilities to those executives. All too frequently, directors take their very membership of the governing body as an affirmation of their 'devotion to the cause'; such directors tend to believe that that devotion can be manifested only by a close involvement with the management systems, and that they must contribute to the tools as well as the objectives.

Often with the best will in the world, such directors may attempt to present their views on particular operational issues. Without effective chairing, therefore, a meeting of the board can easily become a meeting of the executive committee – or even of a project team. This is a phenomenon that is particularly powerful in the voluntary sector. We cannot state too strongly that this is a spurious and improper use of the board process. Any encroachment of this kind into the executive sphere is bad for the senior management/employees connection as well as for the CEO/directors connection. The effect can only be to leave employees genuinely confused as to their true lines of reporting. Of course, anyone is entitled to hear a suggestion being made by another and then do nothing about it; unfortunately, the capacity of an employee of a not-for-profit to do this is limited by virtue of the directors' status.

It is worth reinforcing the point that none of the issues raised in this chapter will be resolved without a chair who has a clear view of the board's role and his/her responsibilities within it, and a capacity to deliver effectively on that clarity of vision. The issues we have identified will not solve themselves. They require leadership. That leadership must be collective, but driven by the chair. To this end, we cannot improve on Andrew Hind's 'Specimen Job Description for the Chair of the Trustees', from his *Governance and Management of Trustees*, which is reproduced as Figure 7.1.

Many directors genuinely take their role as being both to set objectives and to superintend their achievement. What they fail to envisage is a worst-case scenario, in which plans and their implementation have gone awry. How is accountability to be portioned out in such circumstances? The capacity for tension and finger-pointing is considerable if *both* the executive *and* the governance arms of the organisation have become involved in operational matters. In such circumstances, if directors believe that they are accountable for tools as well as objectives, they will be inclined to involve themselves further in management processes so as to 'ensure' improved results. The outcome, foreseeable by any dispassionate observer, is a continual round of directors becoming more and more sucked into a vortex. The effects of their trying to control operations increasingly weaken their capacity to review strategic objectives and their attainment.

In corporate governance terms, it can be disastrous for directors to be concerned to such an extent with tools and processes that they monitor these instead of strategic objectives. In addition, many directors think that, notwithstanding the peculiar duties of the governance role, it is safe – even natural – to carry them out in the breach. We do not mean to downplay the temptations presented to boards to stray beyond the governance role. However, we do urge not-for-profit boards to stipulate unambiguously what directors' responsibilities are. Each organisation should produce an uncomplicated responsibility formulation – a brief or remit – to act as the foundation for its processes. Such a document should go hand-in-hand with some principles aimed at defining the parameters of directors' true functions.

The stewardship responsibility

An effective statement of the directors' remit needs to state explicitly whose interests they exist to serve. It is essential that directors' broad stewardship duties be set down from first principles.

Primary objective

Provide overall leadership to the charity, in close co-operation with the chief executive, in a manner which maximises the contribution of trustees and staff alike and ensures that all involved remain focused on achieving the charity's mission.

Specific duties

Ensure that the trustee board functions effectively by:

- Identifying the skills and experience required on the board
- Seeking new trustees from diverse sources
- Establishing clear procedures for the re-election and retirement of trustees
- Developing a succession plan
- Establishing an appropriate subcommittee structure
- Chairing meetings efficiently through the use of carefully structured agenda and briefing papers and encouraging participation from all trustees.

Ensure that trustees understand their responsibilities by:

- Using trustee job descriptions
- Arranging comprehensive trustee induction and training programmes
- Ensuring that trustees review both the performance of the board as a whole and their own individual contribution annually
- Establishing a governance and management model for the charity.

Ensure that the charity plans strategically by:

- Working closely with the chief executive to ensure that there is clarity about the charity's mission at all levels in the organisation
- Ensuring that management effort is effectively directed within a framework of clearly stated corporate strategies and key tasks.

Ensure that the boundaries of management authority are clearly defined, in particular by:

- Performing a role analysis exercise with the chief executive to ensure that both parties understand the other's role
- Ensuring that a financial policy framework is established within which management can be given freedom to manage the charity's operations
- Ensuring that a performance evaluation process is established
- Ensuring that the chief executive is clear about the key performance indicators that the trustees wish to use to monitor management's performance and by which they will bold the chief executive accountable
- Analysing the particular risk factors inherent in the charity's activities and establishing whether exceptional arrangements for trustee involvement should be instituted in some areas which override the normal trustee governance perspective
- Ensuring that the trustees have issued clear guidelines on areas where varying judgements could be applied. For instance with regard to investment policy, the treatment of earmarked funds held in trust for beneficiaries, equal opportunity practice in staff recruitment, etc.

Other responsibilities

- Appraise the chief executive's performance annually
- Have an involvement in recruitment of senior staff
- Ensure that senior staff are appropriately remunerated
- Promote the charity to its public audience in so far as this assists the chief executive's public relations strategy.

Figure 7.1 Specimen job description for a chair of trustees

Here the particular characteristics of the voluntary arena come into play. That arena is not characterised by the usual unfettered intercourse of a customer as a purchaser of goods or services and a company as a seller of same. So it is necessary in a voluntary organisation for the directors to exercise the market disciplines that ensure the quality of the 'goods' being passed on to the client. We emphasise that not-for-profit directors are stewards of their associations' performance for society in general and for their particular consumers. In the first place, they must protect the clients' well-being and act on their behalf to ensure the value of the 'goods' they are receiving. This is an ethical obligation. In the second place, they must protect the association's solvency and must oversee the ways in which management deploys resources in attempting to carry out the association's role. This is a financial and statutory obligation. This latter kind of stewardship is familiar to the vast majority of directors in the voluntary sector. The same cannot be said for the first type of stewardship.

The first job of not-for-profit directors should be to ensure that the well-being of their clients is being enhanced. This job is less likely to be carried out if directors show an overriding concern with fiscal issues. The board is a vehicle for *policy* setting and monitoring. To the extent that it weakens its focus on that role – by encroaching, for example, on the duties of senior managers – to that extent it is derelict in carrying out its ethical stewardship role. But whose body *is* a voluntary association, which has no stock to sell and no investors to whom it is responsible? We suggest that the association's clients, not its directors or benefactors or employees, are its true 'proprietors'. If directors operate on this assumption, they are more likely to see that they have distinct obligations to benefactors and clients. They will therefore note that they have varying orders of duty. Here a critical and peculiar feature of the not-for-profit board emerges. If 'proprietorship' resides with the clients, then directors' first responsibility is to ensure that their decisions are in the proprietors' interests.

The corollary of this is that directors' ties with the organisation's employees are less important than their ties with clients. Such a hierarchy may be problematic for some employees, not least employees seeking to have the governing body act as the senior executive layer. It will be even more problematic for employees who view the directors as rubber stamps endorsing the decisions of the senior executives and thereby ceding policy responsibility to them. None of this is to gainsay the importance of others with an interest in the organisation. Benefactors are obviously critical – no matter how focused a board is on carrying out its ethical stewardship, it can actually *do* very little about it without benefactors. It should go without saying that the directors' protection of the association's fiscal well-being is a key responsibility. Their central task here, however, is to assure themselves that the operating processes are functioning properly, having first laid down the principles under which those processes should be managed.

So there is a serious, and perhaps unique, recruitment and selection issue for directors of voluntary organisations. Whereas in the commercial sector, one of the criteria for choosing non-executive directors is often their expertise in particular disciplines – marketing, information technology, law and so on – this can almost be dangerous for a not-for-profit board. Certainly it needs to be managed. In our view, the key criteria in selecting directors for such boards should be a capacity to understand and act in accordance with the peculiar stewardship requirements of this sector; to see that the clients are the 'proprietors'; and to be able to contribute to the setting of clear policy directions.

Setting direction

Not-for-profit boards need clear and agreed processes for setting objectives and for overseeing progress against these objectives. It is essential that directors confine themselves to the broad outlines of principles and direction. The board's focus is the What; management's focus is the How, When, Who and How Much.

The purpose of the board's direction-setting is to give itself the capacity to carry out its governance function properly. Often a not-for-profit board will have only one executive member. His or her role, therefore, is critical, as is a common understanding of the nature of the contributions expected from non-executive and executive board members. If there is only one of the latter, then this person has an important additional role as the proxy among the directors of all the other employees. Away from the board table, of course, he or she is their manager. It is a complex set of relationships to manage. Such an executive is also the board's single immediate direct report: a very common model in the not-for-profit sector. The perceived effectiveness of this individual is therefore critical to the issue that we have raised throughout this chapter – the potentially dangerous confusion of the direction and management roles in this sector. Directors will be less likely to concern themselves directly with operational issues to the extent that they are happy with the managerial performance of their executive colleague.

Central to the not-for-profit board's direction-setting role is its 'legacy' responsibility. Here we are referring to the fact that, for a great many organisations in this sector, the customers are permanent, even if the managers and directors are not. In these cases, an important element of directors' stewardship role is the obligation to keep the association extant and vital. This legacy responsibility is especially powerful for the body which alone provides a group of consumers with a particular form of assistance. But it is true as well in cases where the association is not a monopoly provider. Not-for-profit directors in these circumstances too have a peculiar duty to see to the association's durability. Therefore, they need to focus particularly on any potential environmental threats to the association's endurance. This task is complicated somewhat by the fact that, on many governing bodies in this sector, there is a strong likelihood of an ideals mismatch. Given the selection methods often employed in this sector, directors on the same governing body can have quite divergent motives for taking their seats around the table.

The corporate governance consequence of this is that different directors can bring to board deliberations quite different understandings of the association's ideals. It is essential that some consolidation of corporate ideals be achieved. This should be the product of a process of recognition and discussion by directors. Openness is critical here – ideals mismatches cannot be left unresolved. Absent such a reduction, they can turn into highly dysfunctional personal missions. In such circumstances, the *corporate* mission of the organisation will almost become forgotten. The recruitment issue here is that many not-for-profit directors with particular sector knowledge in fact frequently reflect, not the customers, but the sponsors. This can give rise not only to an ideals mismatch but also to significant differences in directors' capacities. These problems are compounded by the fact that the not-for-profit sector contains virtually no examples of governing bodies engaging in the kinds of evaluation practices that we discussed in Chapter 3. Perhaps the key gap is the absence of a template for not-for-profit boards – this chapter has been an attempt to fill that gap.

Above all, we believe that the principles of good corporate governance pertain across all sectors. It is remarkable that many experienced directors and managers from the business sector, when they first take a not-for-profit board seat, allow themselves to be persuaded that the voluntary sector has nothing in common with any others. That is an untrue and quite debilitating attitude struck by too many voluntary sector professionals. It is debilitating because its effect, at the level of corporate governance, is to have those board members who could genuinely add governance value, not to do so. It is difficult to see how the organisation or its clients benefit from this outcome.

8 Communication

Setting the scene

The corporate sector in particular must not only have strong governance standards effectively in place but it must also be seen to have these standards in place. Just as leaders are assessed for congruity between their stated message and their actions, the same is true with corporations. Leaders know full well that to be effective they need to have clear goals with a simple message clearly and constantly communicated to their target audience. The task of communication is a priority and a time-demanding one, as most business people can attest. It requires presentational skills which need to be developed, planning to produce a coherent communications programme and constancy of delivery to ensure that the message is heard. Most corporations, as well as non-profit enterprises, recognise the need to communicate to their constituents, but – at least in the corporate sector – it is unusual for much time to be spent communicating the issues of corporate governance. Indeed, the centrality of effort is around direct shareholder interest matters such as corporate strategy, financial performance, managerial competence and commercially specific issues such as brand awareness. Governance is typically dealt with in a formal way in the annual report or on an ad hoc basis in responding to press questions or criticisms as they arise.

One would think, in this modern age, that it would be simplicity itself to use the new technology-led avenues to communicate, and that this would make life easier for the busy leader. Alas, this is not true. Not only are some forms of media such as television demanding; leaders also need to deal with increasingly sophisticated and usually aggressive media people as well as with a more knowledgeable audience. Therefore, the communicator needs to be clear about the appropriate vehicle by which the message is best transmitted and needs to be competent to effectively share the message in that media form. The range of choice is wide, including direct contact with small groups or large audiences, radio, newspapers, magazines, television, cable or satellite options, electronic mail and other points of access on the global information highway. The wide choice of media channels available and the bombardment of

151

messages on the general public provides an additional challenge to gain effectiveness of the message given the clutter it is surrounded with. The pressure then is for the message to be clearly presented in a simple way, which of course has the potential disadvantage of being narrow and thin in content. This last point gives a great opportunity for mischievous reporting either by ridiculing the simple statement or turning this on its head and constructing a logic form based on populist half-truths.

Knockers

Over the past decade in particular, society has grown an increasing crop of 'knockers' – those people in society who delight to find the negative even in the best achievements. This attitude, more prevalent in societies such as Britain than in the USA, is not just the product of envy of 'the haves', and neither is it voiced solely by the dispossessed. We have spawned a view, exemplified in the media, that the good or positive is passé (or even suspect) and that the stumbling of the great, news of disaster or poking a finger in the eye of tradition is newsworthy, as well as great fun.

Perhaps one should not be too surprised by this trend given the increasing ease of information flow across communities. The very concept of privacy has gone. It is now easy and broadly acceptable to publicly transmit the most personal or private details of people. Naturally enough, the populace at large love to see that leaders have 'feet of clay' and therefore royalty, politicians, community leaders, business leaders and hierarchy in the church are all amongst the target group for media hounds.

The fact that the media of today allows for speedy charges to be made in a form that may well be incomplete or inconclusive yet escapes legal redress through the courts, destroys any mystique surrounding such leaders. Leadership is losing respect. Not only is this a personal issue for those who lead but it is also an important lesson for corporations and institutions. Defensive communication on governance or standards is not enough. A positive communication programme must be set down.

Wider reputation

It is easy to see how lapses in standards of governance can damage a wider reputation. If a company relies on the support of the community at large because they are its customers, and promotes a policy of wholesome values, it must constantly guard its reputation. Such a company is Marks

& Spencer Plc which has an enviable record of achievement for its shareholders. It achieves this success not only through its reputation for quality and value for money, but in a setting where other stakeholders such as its customers, workforce and suppliers are treated fairly. It sets its suppliers minimum standards which it must maintain in its factories, and minimum conditions for the workers employed there. It lays out minimum quality standards and process standards that are compatible with the company's reputation for quality and which are compatible with the environment. Employees are well aware of the need for service to their customers, are equipped with appropriate product knowledge and are encouraged to provide practical help in the community in which they work.

When this reputation is attacked in the media, such as the example in January 1996 when Granada Television made allegations of the use of child labour in M&S suppliers' factories and also of mis-labelling the products with the wrong country of origin, it is not surprising that M&S defended strongly. However, any such defensive posture needs also to be coupled with a positive communication that continues to reinforce in the constituents' minds the company's positive community involvement and the living examples of its high standards in action.

Areas of concern

We have already illustrated the areas in which the public at large might be expected to raise legitimate questions of governance. To summarise the main areas of concern:

- Are the controls and standards in the organisation appropriate to protect values and net assets?
- Are there effective controls and is there appropriate segregation to ensure that management are achieving appropriate goals?
- Does the company have a pay and benefits policy for its executives which is appropriate and in keeping with peer groups and results?
- Are there satisfactory corporate goals which are compatible with legitimate aspirations of other stakeholders?
- Does the company have high ethical standards that meet reasonable community expectations?

Especially in the corporate sector, attention needs to be given to these concerns. A programme of communication is really essential. Of course, the message being sent must be credible and therefore backed up by the deeds of the company and its leaders. The message must be comprehensible and consistent. Central to effective leadership is effective communication of the message.

Managing the message

Basic rules

There are some basic rules. The first is that one needs to be quite clear on what the message really is. In a simple form the message must have clarity and believability. It should also be appropriate and not sidetrack into issues that are not central to the main thrust of the argument. Second, the style as well as the content needs to be pitched to the relevant audience. A presentation to the workforce is likely to be different from one that is appropriate for shareholders. Third, the deliverer of the message needs to choose the most appropriate media vehicle to transmit the message to the target audience. For example, where an argument is complex and needs to be built up to a conclusion, print is more important than television where arguments are often condensed to a shortened, more pithy form. Fourth, in setting out the communication, special thought must be given to other interest groups to avoid conflicts with other stakeholders, or inappropriate timing. As an example, it is insensitive in the extreme for a company to announce a new, additional long-term incentive plan for top management at a time of a significant redundancy programme within the company.

Many institutions, companies included, cannot understand why they do not appear to get a fair hearing from the media when some challenge to their reputation or standing is made. There may be a number of reasons for this. First and, in our view, most important, leaders cannot regard the press as a 'fair weather friend'. They cannot expect empathetic treatment in these moments if they have not taken the trouble to build up a relationship with the key media elements over time. It is time-consuming work which often has no tangible immediate return for such time invested. Yet it is important to make this investment. Second, like it or not, some corporations are headed up by media-unfriendly people who lead with their chin and set up themselves and their organisations for attack by the press. The combination of environmentally friendly products and an abrasive Anita Roddick gives a challenge to the press to highlight real or perceived chinks in Body Shop's persona. There are corporate and political leaders who show disdain for the media, who in turn delight in getting their own back on those people when circumstances permit. Third – there is little that boards can do about this – many journalists are personally hostile to capitalism and all its works.

If the media believes that a leader displays some of the following qualities he or she is likely to be negatively treated:

- arrogance (intellectual or social)
- disdainful of the media
- dismissive
- unavailable, especially on important issues
- insensitive to other groups in society
- snobbish
- unduly abrasive
- 'holier than thou' – in which case the media will take delight in demonstrating a lack of congruence between ideals and actions.

While most leaders would not immediately attribute any or many of the above qualities to themselves, the sad fact is that others may hold a different view. The strong message that flows from this is that executives who deal with the public had better know themselves well, see their weaknesses as well as their strengths through the eyes of the public at large and then undertake training programmes to make step improvements. One of the best ways of achieving this is through video-taped media training where a really experienced trainer puts the executive through his or her paces. It is a sobering learning experience to see the output on tape and to see oneself as others do! There then follows the challenge of self-improvement through a combination of plenty of practice and tutoring by trained people.

Coping with the unexpected

As sure as night follows day, even the best of organisations or the most talented of leaders will need to cope with an unexpected or one-off event that requires a strong response. When allegations are made against, say, a corporation that holds strong values, an appropriate response needs to be made. Naturally, the allegations themselves are important as well as the way they are asserted and the media form used. Sometimes, the right response may well be to do nothing because a continuation of the debate may be counter-productive, giving credence to a hostile pressure group and its claims.

The first natural response when this happens is to get really angry at the unbalanced, unjustified claims made in usually an emotive way. This is understandable but it is not a good basis for drawing up the best action plan. As Aristotle, in the third century BC observed, 'Anyone can become angry – that is easy. But to be angry with the right person, to the right degree, at the right time, for the right purpose and in the right way – this is not easy.'

Perhaps in the great majority of cases it is essential to respond appropriately to try and protect the important reputation of the company concerned. In extreme cases, the final remedy may well be found in the courts, yet even taking this action requires additional good communication. If an element of the media is going to run a story of potential negative consequences then it is important to decide how best to respond. Experience shows that it is usually best to participate, to try and ameliorate the damage, ensuring at least some chance of putting the opposing point of view. Seldom does a refusal to comment go down well with the audience.

A recent case study can be seen with Marks & Spencer who were mentioned earlier in this chapter. They were attacked on what appears to us to be very flimsy information on two *World in Action* programmes produced by Granada Television. Granada alleged that one supplier to that retailer had used 'child labour' in one overseas factory and that some products made in Morocco had been wrongly labelled in the United Kingdom. During the preparation for the programme, M&S responded fully to those allegations, pointing out that:

- The factory had been inspected independently by government officials, by M&S and by the supplier and no under-age employees were found.
- The mis-labelling was an error of that one named supplier (Desmonds) covering only a small number of garments.

M&S also provided a main board director to appear on the first programme to refute the allegations. The first programme was produced in a way that M&S believed to be biased and made allegations that were untrue. Given that this went to the core of their values, they declined to participate in the second programme on alleged design copying and issued a writ against Granada. They also circulated all shareholders, all account holders and put up notices in each of their stores making their position clear. The letter to shareholders is shown in Figure 8.1. This action was totally appropriate and is an example of coping with the unexpected in the field of communication.

There is another aspect of dealing with the unexpected that reinforces the case for good governance as the norm. A company that has put in place the basic tenets of governance and that has communicated effectively will have a more fertile ground on which to grow support if it receives an unexpected attack. This is especially true in the case of a company takeover where the defending company must make its case to its shareholder base to maintain independence. While the overriding evidence will be the economic judgement of value for the shareholders over time and not just at the moment of the bid, shareholders will also be influenced by the track record of governance.

Take for example the case of Granada Plc bidding for Forte. The latter company was perceived to have had a mediocre to poor record of providing adequate returns for its shareholders and to have less effective management than Granada. It had also shown little regard for best practice in governance and its communication with the City was not of a high standard. Prior to the bid, Forte had commenced strengthening the board through the appointment of quality non-executives. During the contested bid, Forte also promised a much more focused strategy with the disposal of non-core hotel businesses. It was, however, not until the last couple of weeks of the bid that the Chairman/Chief Executive role occupied by Sir Rocco Forte was split. This was regarded by the City as coming too late and only undertaken as an appeasement necessary for independence.

While the City no doubt made its decision based on their understanding of the economics, they were influenced strongly by the overall quality of the respective managements which included their adherence to principles of good governance. Forte were on the back foot in needing to launch a comprehensive campaign to shareholders and the press when they were perceived as having a track record that was less than adequate in this area.

When there is a hostile bid there is a need to build the campaign and the communication of this message, which is much more difficult if this has not previously been a priority. Another example of this is seen with Coats Viyella in 1991 when it made a hostile bid for Tootal following a period of stalemate and Tootal rejecting Coats Viyella's overtures. Coats Viyella had not previously bothered much with the City or the communication of its plans and the actions it took were seen as a bit of a surprise.

MARKS & SPENCER

REGISTERED OFFICE: MICHAEL HOUSE . BAKER STREET . LONDON W1A 1DN
FACSIMILE: 0171-487 2679 . CABLES: MARSPENZA LONDON . TELEX: 267141
TELEPHON: 0171-935 4422

12 January 1996

Dear Shareholder

We want to inform you personally that Marks & Spencer has issued a writ in the High Court against Granada Television Limited in respect of the very serious allegations made in the World In Action Programme screened at 8.00pm on 8 January 1996.

The programme claimed that Marks & Spencer knowingly and deliberately exploited child labour in order to boost profits and also that the company deliberately misled customers by the incorrect labelling of country of origin on St Michael products.

Marks & Spencer has also issued separate proceedings against News Group Newspapers Limited in respect of an article which appeared in the News of the World on 7 January 1996 and which contained the same allegations.

These outrageous claims are totally untrue and constitute a most serious attack on the integrity and reputation of your Company.

The Board would like to reassure you that both legal actions will be vigorously pursued.

We will keep you informed of further developments and in the meantime we would like to thank you for your continued loyalty and support.

Yours sincerely

Deputy Chairman

FOR AND ON BEHALF OF
THE BOARD OF DIRECTORS

StMichael

THE BRAND NAME OF MARKS AND SPENCER p.l.c.
REGISTERED NO. 214436 (ENGLAND AND WALES)

Figure 8.1   M&S letter to shareholders

The bid received the support of the shareholder base only because the strategy was credible, value was available and a new management team installed at the end of 1990 saw communication with the City as a continuing priority. They started from well behind and had to work very hard on their own shareholder base as well as the top Tootal shareholders to get their support for the hostile bid, which was successful.

The annual report

Remuneration

The Greenbury Committee made it clear that companies had to show greater transparency of remuneration policy and payments made to directors in their annual reports. This committee highlighted the importance of the remuneration committee of the boards of listed companies. It recognised the progress in disclosures in annual reports of recent years but then set down both some minimum standards in the code of best practice and in addition some points for further debate.

The code of best practice requires a report of the remuneration committee in the annual report which has the following features:

- Policies on executive remuneration to be clearly set out.
- Details of each director's remuneration should be separately set out with an analysis of salary, annual bonus and long-term incentive plan benefits.
- Details of pension entitlements actually earned by directors. Given that there are a number of ways that this can be measured, it was also recommended that the Institute of Actuaries should give a lead on the most appropriate measure to adopt.
- Details of earnings or potential earnings from executive share options.
- Income from taxable benefits.
- Details of the length of directors' service contracts. The Greenbury Committee observed that there is a strong case for one-year service contracts.

Codes of best practice are one aspect and companies will also need to meet the listing requirements for the Stock Exchange as well as comply with the Companies Act. In the United Kingdom the 1985 Companies Act sets out legal requirements in part I of schedule 6 to that Act. In summary, the most important items are:

- the total of directors' emoluments including pension contributions
- emoluments (excluding pension contributions) of the chairman and the highest paid director where this is not the chairman
- a list showing the number of directors in each income band.

Comparative figures for the previous year are also required.

Prior to the Greenbury Committee, the Cadbury Code also had its code of best practice. Basically, Cadbury required disclosure of the directors' total emoluments and those of the chairman and the highest paid director. Included under this code were salary and bonus, pension contributions and stock options. The distinction of salary payments from performance-related payments was clearly recommended as well as an explanation of the basis on which performance-measured pay is made.

The challenge for the board of directors is how to cope with these demands in a positive, responsive, informative way with a clarity of communication that leaves the reader with the real essence of what is happening with top pay and conditions. This challenge is made stronger when companies also endeavour to logically include information on directors' shareholdings in the same section of the report. The issue of clarity is a real one given that some schemes are not simple to explain or may well vary for different levels of management. The vexed question of pension fund contributions and how to express this is complex and has a number of different alternatives. Many forests may be cut down to provide the paper to meet the recommended disclosures, which will not, however, provide much advance in clarity or understanding!

Pension funds

The law is clear that the employing organisation has the economic responsibility to fund the liabilities to meet the promised benefits for its members. Equally, it is accepted that any actuarial surplus in the fund is for the benefit of the company or other employing body if this is outside the corporate arena. The state of the funding of the pension fund and the implications of this need to be correctly reflected in the statement of accounts.

What is not so straightforward is how to respond to the Greenbury Committee's recommendation on disclosure. In some cases there is a defined contribution scheme and the recipient receives the accumulation of the contributions from the company, his own and the value of the asset acception over the lifetime of this fund. Here, it is straightforward and pretty much universally agreed that the amount the employer sets aside each year and pays into this fund is the correct cost of pension. However, in the other case where an employee receives a defined benefit based on service and ending salary, the position is much more complex.

At present there appear to be five options which are being considered by the Institute of Actuaries:

Method 1   *cash contribution* which uses the overall scheme contribution rate.

Method 2   *accrued benefit* which is the difference between the *amount* of the leaving service benefits at the start and end of the year.

Method 3   *transfer value*, being the difference in the *value* of the leaving service benefits at the start and end of the year. (This is the method recommended by the Actuaries to implement Greenbury proposals.)

Method 4   *SSAP24 basis* for calculating the cost of the accruing benefits.

Method 5   *notional funding* basis for calculating the cost of the accruing benefits.

Each method has its own advantages and disadvantages. Some are certainly much more complex to understand and explain, especially to lay readers of company reports.

Method 1:   *Cash contribution* is the method currently used by most companies today. It is simple but it does not show the cost of any individuals scheme which is lost in the averaging.

Method 1 is calculated as the group contribution rate actually being paid by the company to the relevant pension scheme, multiplied by the appropriate pensionable remuneration for the director. This really does not help the disclosure case and it is therefore not possible to make comparisons across companies.

Method 2:   *Accrued benefit*. The disclosure would be the change in the accrued benefit over the year and the total accrued benefit at the end of the year. Leaving service benefits would be used for this purpose. Also disclosed would be details needed to evaluate the cost of the benefit, for example the director's age, normal pension age and the entitlement to pension increases. The method is similar to that used in the USA.

This is relatively simple, being based solely on the scheme pension formula. It shows only the director's own pension but gives no indication of associated benefits (e.g. spouse's pension). It is, however, difficult to ascertain the value to the director of the benefits and the cost to the company of providing them.

Example (Method 2)

Pensionable service completed at end of year	10 years
Pensionable remuneration:	
at start of year	£100,000
at end of year	£105,000
Pension actual rate	1/30ths
Accrued benefit at end of year:	

$$\frac{10}{30} \times 105,000 = \qquad\qquad £35,000$$

Change in accrued benefit over year:

$$35,000 - \frac{9}{30} \times 100,000 = \qquad\qquad £5,000$$

(SOURCE: Lane, Clark & Peacock, Actuaries, January 1996.)

Method 3:   *Transfer value.* This preferred method of disclosure would be the difference between the director's accrued benefits at the start and end of the year. Key features are as follows:

- It is relatively simple to calculate and understand. It is the increase in the transfer value available to the director by remaining in the scheme over the year.
- The figures will tend to rise faster as the increasing age of the director has the effect on its own of increasing the value of the benefits.

Method 4: *SSAP24 basis.* This uses the same method and assumptions as are used for calculating the general pension disclosures in the company accounts under the accounting principles that are applicable under SSAP24. For each director individually, the following amounts would be calculated:

- the value of pension accrued during the year
- the effect of the difference between the actual increase in the director's pensionable remuneration over the year and the increase assumed in the calculation basis.

This method is very similar to the fifth one listed below.

Method 5: *Notional funding*. In effect, it is assumed that the director is the sole member of the scheme, with a contribution rate set as a level percentage of his remuneration in order to meet the final remuneration-based benefits at normal pension age. Each year the 'contribution rate' is recalculated to take account of actual changes in remuneration or benefits, but the Consultation Paper does not make clear how this would be done.

Key features of Methods 4 and 5 are as follows:

- They are considerably more complex than the preceding methods, both in application and interpretation.
- The use of SSAP24 in Method 4. This approach is reasonably objective and it should enable meaningful comparisons to be made between different companies.

It will be seen from just this fairly cursory review of methods available to disclose the information foreseen as helpful by the Greenbury Committee, that the area is difficult to understand and difficult to communicate in a clear way. While the actuaries may be clear about the purist way to show information, they are not necessarily expert in how to communicate the essence of this in a comprehensive way. There may well be a case for letting companies deal with the spirit of Greenbury and to communicate the abnormal or essential changes rather than having a uniform straitjacket for all. For example, it is much more meaningful to disclose pension funding cost to the company when there is a significant change in reward patterns. At British Gas, to disclose that the pension cost to deal with a 75 per cent salary increase (while withdrawing non-pensionable performance rewards) is much more important than describing the pension cost calculation over a page or two of text!

Communication and other stakeholders

Whatever the decision, our fear is that the Greenbury good intentions will not be achieved in practice because of the sheer complexity that lies behind the assumptions and methodology of each of the alternatives. While there are attractions to the simple approach of describing the benefits including the years of service needed to attain them, the cost met by the director and the average cost to the company for the fund in total, this will not always show the true picture. It is especially distorting when large increases in salary are granted towards the end of the working life of a director as this has a very heavy funding cost which does not usually get highlighted. This is often lost in the averaging of the total cost to the company of the total fund for all employees.

Criticism is well directed when there are a number of examples of chairmen or chief executives who have a substantial increase in salary, perhaps within the last three years of their service, giving up variable or performance pay and benefits. The funding cost is huge, as British Gas Plc no doubt knows having given its chief executive a 75 per cent uplift in salary in return for reduced bonus opportunity towards the end of his career.

The principles of communication are the same even when the target audience is quite different. A clear, consistent message needs to be imparted throughout the organisation with the communication tailor-made for the specific audience who will have their own agenda, expectations and concerns. Naturally enough, one cannot communicate governance issues in a vacuum or simply on an ad hoc basis. A total programme needs to be in place so that there is a coherence and an understanding of the priorities as well as of the resource requirements.

Many thoughtful and successful businesses have a well thought through programme of communication for internal consumption. They recognise the concept of cascading down information that is relevant and is in sufficient detail appropriate to the audience. We have shown this approach illustrated in Figure 8.2 where the cascading concept can be seen in the different levels within the enterprise. Often, however, the actual implementation of the communication exercise is less than satisfactory, usually as a result of inadequate time and resource.

Figure 8.2 emphasises:

- the integrated nature of the communication plan
- the cascading down through the various levels of a common message that is appropriate for the target audience
- the importance of feedback.

There are many businesses today that do not apply sufficient rigour to their internal programme and, as a consequence, deal reactively with events as they occur. However, even for those more proactive companies with a detailed internal plan of communication there is much more to do. There are the other stakeholders who need to be considered. For illustrative purposes, Figure 8.3 outlines a programme across all stakeholders.

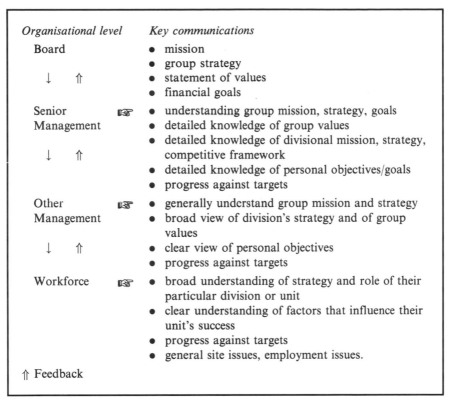

Organisational level		Key communications
Board	↓ ⇑	• mission • group strategy • statement of values • financial goals
Senior Management	☞ ↓ ⇑	• understanding group mission, strategy, goals • detailed knowledge of group values • detailed knowledge of divisional mission, strategy, competitive framework • detailed knowledge of personal objectives/goals • progress against targets
Other Management	☞ ↓ ⇑	• generally understand group mission and strategy • broad view of division's strategy and of group values • clear view of personal objectives • progress against targets
Workforce	☞	• broad understanding of strategy and role of their particular division or unit • clear understanding of factors that influence their unit's success • progress against targets • general site issues, employment issues.
⇑ Feedback		

Figure 8.2 Summarised internal communication programme

Before briefly commenting on the channels for sharing messages with the stakeholders, there is a general issue that impacts all businesses. There is a general torpor within business communities around the world and little effort is taken to communicate the economic value and benefit to society in general that flows from successful business. Within the school system, careers advisors are often poorly prepared to make their constituents aware of the value of business. Equally, there is very little understanding of the relevance of key numbers in reported results. There is then a tendency to dwell on 'bigness' so that profits are looked at in their own right rather than related to the capital base to support them or perhaps to sales levels. Senior directors' salaries will be viewed outside of the comparator base that is relevant and will tend to be viewed in isolation with most comments on absolute size. This is not just a problem of an ill-informed community but also reflects the lack of corporate communication and of education over a long period of time.

Board and senior management

Shareholders	Customers	Workforce	Suppliers	Community
Strategy	Mutual understanding of each other's strategy	Broad understanding of strategy	Mutual understanding of each other's strategy	Company's role and value in local community
Competitive advantage	Shared opportunities and threats	Success factors	Shared opportunities and threats	Company values
Industry trends	Clearly understood expectations	Site progress against targets	Clearly understood expectations	Community support to company
Depth of management performance	Appraisal of performance	Site employment issues	Appraisal of performance	Broad knowledge of industry competitive issues
Significant events	Local community issues			

Figure 8.3 Communication to stakeholders

Without labouring the point more, the best of business firms are continuing with their positive broadly based programme of communication that reflects the needs of the stakeholders in line with Figure 8.2. In summary form, let us see the practical communication devices that successful companies utilise to spread their key messages across the constituent parts of their target audience.

Shareholders

The following communication devices are used to ensure that there is a clear understanding of the company:

- half-yearly presentation in depth of results and achievement of important milestones
- special shareholder events to describe special opportunities, changes or in-depth reviews of part of the group
- analyst special events to focus on some key aspect of the company, e.g. strategy
- annual and half-yearly reports to shareholders that are informative, broadly based and deal openly with issues such as corporate governance, the environment and ethical standards.

Customers and suppliers

Many businesses talk glibly about the partnership that exists between the supplier and their customer. Although those that pay more than lip-service to this concept will have specific programmes for the company's key customers and separately its key suppliers, the principles are very much the same for both. The major piece of groundwork is to establish clearly how each can add value to the other in a 'win-win' situation. This involves an understanding of each other's strategy and implies an openness in sharing sensitive information. It also often needs a culture change from the historic antagonistic buyer/supplier relationship that has characterised relationships in the past.

The communication process usually has the following component parts:

- a preliminary joint study and following meeting to identify mutually beneficial opportunities and how these can be exploited
- an understanding of each other's strategies so that the focus can be on the area of greatest value creation

- laying down an action plan with agreed milestones
- appraisal of performance against the objectives and feedback of the learning that follows from this.

Workforce

Figure 8.2 shows the areas where communication is best directed. The vehicles used in the process include:

- the annual report, often in an employees' version that gives fewer simpler key messages without the distraction of the legal requirements of a full annual report
- site briefings by senior directors who will talk in a general sense about corporate issues and set the tune for the more intimate plant or worker group briefings
- European Works Councils which allow for two-way pan-European communication;
- company newspapers, corporate orders and written policies.

The community

A company is an integral part of the community both in its own right and through its employees. There is a strong case to be made to ensure that the community is aware of the value that is created by the business enterprises that reside within it. Too often companies assume that there is ready recognition of the economic value created within a broad community and that there is a broad support for it. The company must be a good citizen, and the best 'citizens' encourage their employees to participate in the broader community affairs. Company community-based communication programmes will:

- ensure that their efforts in support of charities and good causes are recognised and appreciated through the judicious use of local publicity
- highlight appropriately many different ways in which the community is being supported, e.g. scholarships, employment opportunities, training programmes.

When such a broadly based proactive approach to communication is adopted there is a much more receptive audience to hear bad news should it come, or for a more informed discussion on matters of broad governance. The value of this positive climate is very high, as issues can be addressed based on their merits. Where change is required, one can move more speedily forward without the frustration of taking considerable time to prepare the recipients before specific plans can be implemented.

Importance of coherence

We would like to conclude this chapter on a more general but important theme. There is a question for society in general that is posed as a result of the current preoccupation of the media and indeed of society with the negative, with knocking of institutions and leadership in general. It is counterproductive to dwell on negatives and destroy the inter-community trust that is tenuously in place at present. This approach creates issues where essentially none exist and is divisive of the community. There is no doubt in our mind that this approach which is common in our times, weakens leadership and, indeed, sub-optimises the benefits for society.

To take an example, whatever one's personal views of Bill Clinton as President of the United States, the continual personal sniping at his and Hillary Clinton's private lives weakens his authority and demeans the office of President of the United States of America. This principle is equally true in other dimensions of the community as well as of business leadership. The worst scenario is that, given this antagonism, this failure to applaud the positive and recognise significant contributions, there will be fewer people prepared to expose themselves to the demands of leadership. When media crusades step over the line of objective reporting and turn into witch hunts there is a cost to society that is cumulative with each attack. We are unlikely to see such a display in other economies such as Singapore or Malaysia, to pick two of the 'tiger' economies that outperform most of the West. Even in Europe, such an approach is less likely to be found in countries with a greater sense of chauvinism such as France and Germany which therefore disadvantages those who tacitly applaud such negative attacks.

We believe that there is an important task of ensuring that at all levels communication with society is positive and shows the achievements within the system that are delivered by leaders in the private and public sector. This is not a case to make them immune to criticism but is a strong plea for better balance in the community. In our view, this is an aspect of both leadership and responsibility of each section of society.

In this chapter we have shown the central importance of communication both as a positive contributor to good governance and to ensure that different interest groups are aware of the setting, the objectives and the achievement. Pitching the story in the right way, to the right audience and through the right media form are all contributors to success or failure of communication. Leaders often have a less than clear view of their intrinsic ability to communicate and this is an important area for development. Looking forward, communication will be of even greater importance. This fact must make building this skill base a priority for all who would be successful in the period ahead.

9 Summary and Conclusions

Governance and ethical values

Running throughout this book is the theme that governance adds real value to an organisation and that for it to be effective the standards laid down must be practised in spirit and be part of the ethos of the body concerned. All senior managers, including directors, need to have standards that are compatible with the values of the company and be satisfied that their own reputation is enhanced rather than diminished in their work setting. Professional managers, especially at senior levels, have as their most important asset their reputation which must be protected by holding appropriate ethical and professional values.

The ethical issues that directors may address can range from the purpose of the organisation to the individual's degree of comfort with its actions. This can be just as true for not-for-profits as for companies. Individuals may need to decide, for example, if they can remain in a corporation or industry in which health and safety regulations are not enthusiastically implemented. Even prior to having to address such questions, other individuals will need to ask themselves if they are prepared to accept a board position in an industry whose products or services may be ethically questionable.

At board level, directors need to feel that they are satisfied with the overall governance environment, including the provision of appropriate information. Our case study of Genesis Plc in Chapter 2 clearly highlights the dilemma that Brian Ball felt about the situation be saw there. He was also uncomfortable about the position he was put in and he continued to worry about whether he should have been more public about his resignation.

While directors and others on governing bodies of non-profit-making organisations will have an agenda of items that ask questions to test the ethical values held, a checklist is a helpful aide-memoir. We have included in Figure 9.1 sample questions about the organisation's ethical values which is reproduced from the Institute of Canadian Accountants publication *Governance Processes for Control*. This is a helpful generic list that should prompt the appropriate level of thinking.

(To be addressed by directors and the board; those marked * may need to be discussed without the directors who are also members of management.)

For the individual director on a continuing basis

- Am I personally comfortable with the organisation's mission, vision and strategy? And with its actions, proposals and values? Are they consistent with my own sense of what is right?
- Do I ensure I get all the information I need to exercise my judgement?
- Have I identified and disclosed conflicts of interest?
- Is the CEO responding in a forthright manner to board questions? *
- Does the conduct of the CEO and other senior management personnel, inside and outside the organisation, set an appropriate example? *

For the board's consideration

- Has the board approved a suitable code of conduct for the organisation? Does the board monitor the implementation of the code and the need for updating it in light of changes in the organisation's activities and society's expectations?
- Is the board's own conduct consistent with that code?
- Does the board take the time to consider whether proposals presented for approval are 'right' for the organisation and consistent with its ethical values?
- Does the board act in the best interest of the organisation, whether this interest conflicts or coincides with the best interest of a particular shareholder?
- Does the board receive appropriate reports from management on matters relating to ethical conduct such as environmental protection, employee health and safety, human rights, improper payments and conflicts of interest?
- Does the board receive from management a report on the results of monitoring compliance with the organisation's code of conduct?
- Has the board asked the internal and external auditors to bring to its attention any proposal or action of which they are aware that they believe is inconsistent with the organisation's code of conduct?
- Can the board trust the CEO and other senior management personnel to act with integrity? *

SOURCE: Canadian Institute of Chartered Accountants, *Governance Processes for Control*, Nov. 1995.

Figure 9.1 Sample questions about the organisation's ethical values

Value of governance

We hold the view that corporate governance is very much about adding value. Companies and other enterprises with a professional and positive attitude to governance are stronger and have a greater record of achievement. Indeed, some company directors, like Allen Sykes, in his article 'Proposals for Internationally Competitive Corporate Governance in Britain and America', suggest that there is an important direct relationship between a country's corporate governance system and its economic success.

Certainly, there is a wide body of opinion that recognises the value-adding role of governance and most would accept that at the very least a satisfactory governance system is about stopping value from being subtracted from an enterprise. Some hazards or risks can be avoided with an appropriate approach to risk analysis. This will lead to a strong, effective control environment. But governance is not just about controls and restrictions. It is really about creating an environment of enterprise and best professional practice to extract the maximum long term-value from a commercial enterprise.

However, not everyone agrees with this. Some still see the requirements of the various codes as being bureaucratic and restrictive. They look to the letter of the law to see what they need to do to get the compliance ticks from the auditors who monitor the code. Lord Young, formerly Chairman of Cable and Wireless Plc, was negative about these codes at the Institute of Directors Conference on Enterprise and Governance which was held in London in October 1995. He was reported as saying, 'I believe that the combination of Cadbury and Greenbury will be as helpful as the Social Chapter of the Maastricht Treaty itself and very much for the self-same reason. When I look at all the additional bureaucracy I have to go through on my board, often following the form rather than the substance, often ticking boxes rather than doing anything meaningful, I begin to wonder what all this originally set out to prevent.' Others at the conference were more focused on the spirit of good governance rather than the letter of regulation.

Private company

Throughout much of this book we have focused on the opportunities to improve value through good governance in larger and public corporations. We have also demonstrated that the same basic principles apply to non-profit-making enterprises and also to smaller businesses. It is helpful to dwell on the private company. It requires much the same disciplines in its control environment and a culture in which high standards are valued. We are well aware of many privately owned companies where non-executive directors are appointed and add value through adopting much the same principles that apply to public companies that we have advocated in this book. The board needs to understand its own role, to set standards, agree strategy, annual plans and succession plans. Equally, it needs to monitor the progress of the company and its chief executive. These iterative processes give assurance to shareholders and to other stakeholders that the company is not unduly inward-looking.

It is also instructive to look at the challenge and opportunity that confronts a privately owned company which intends to make a public début on the Stock Exchange. We have included as a case study Barnes Engineering Plc, a family company that transferred to the second generation of the family and needed to go public (Case Study 9.1). This is a familiar pattern in Europe and the United States where companies are successful as private concerns but for a variety of reasons need to break out of this family mould into public share ownership. Sometimes, this is due to the end of a dynasty and resultant differing family objectives about the future. Especially in the case of those who are not directly involved in the management, it is prudent to spread the family's investments beyond this one company. Sometimes, the management understand that the conditions for their success are changing and a more global strategy may be needed. The need for fresh capital may also be a factor in future expansion. Whatever the scene, we would strongly argue that a tight focus on good governance adds significant value to shareholders in these circumstances. The case study, 'A letter to the chairman', highlights some of the decision areas for a private company wishing to go public. John Barnes had approached one of the authors of this book to help him think through the issues of governance in taking his private company into the public sector.

Reflections

There is value in pausing to reflect on the key messages and observations made in earlier chapters of this book.

Research

Our research gives some interesting insights and food for thought which influence our thinking and input to the model for change which will be

——— **Case Study 9.1**———

A letter to the chairman

Barnes Engineering Plc (a private company about to go public)

Background

Barnes Engineering Plc is an illustrative company based in the UK with sales of £100m, an operating profit of £8m and assets of £40m. Because the business has expanded rapidly over the past three years since John Barnes assumed control following the death of his father, it has needed cash for expansion. In consequence, it is quite highly geared with borrowings of £25m. The interest payable was a little over £2.5m leaving a pre-tax profit of £5.5m. This is very profitable compared with Barnes Engineering's competition due to the specialty high-precision nature of its products, and this, together with the exceptional service the company offers, has been responsible for its recent rapid growth. John Barnes bought out the shares owned by his father (previously 75 per cent) so that John and his immediate family now own all of the shares. However, they also have personal debt approaching £10m which they wish to reduce. They have been advised that the company should be floated with 40 per cent of the shareholding put into public hands and that this would raise about £15m. This should then be followed by a further public issue to reduce the company debt burden and to fund new growth.

John Barnes has always run the company as he sees fit. There are no non-executive directors but regular board meetings are held with John chairing the meeting which is attended by the Finance, Sales and Production Directors as well as the Company Secretary who is his wife. There are no board committees. He is very aware that Barnes Engineering Plc as it moves to the next phase of its development needs a more formal base of governance which is why he asked for advice on what steps to put in place. Here is the letter sent to him.

Dear John,

First of all, you should recognise that there are fundamental differences between the present situation and the proposed public status in which, say, 40 per cent of the shares will be held by the general public. To summarise these changes, I would highlight the following:

- You are no longer sole owner and manager therefore you will need to separate these roles in your mind and in your actions.
- Private, family transactions must be totally excluded from the company and decisions must be taken on an arm's length basis where you and the company are involved.
- Management must always act in the best interests of all shareholders and must be committed to securing the long-term addition of value for all shareholders.
- The board must be independent and seen to be capable of acting independently. It must monitor the management and its effectiveness and give confidence to outside shareholders.
- The shareholders and other stakeholders should be assured that the control environment is strong and that the accounts can be relied upon as a true and fair statement of the company's position.

Therefore, with this background, there are a number of issues that you will need to address. In order to give confidence to outside investors, the first thing you will need is a board that has preferably three independent non-executive directors. This will provide the major part of the assurance that is required. However, you will also need to ensure that there are sufficient checks and balances in place to satisfy the shareholders that you, as major shareholder and decision-maker, do not have unfettered power. Ideally, the shareholders would like to see the roles of chairman and chief executive split with an independent, non-executive chairman taking over that role. This would represent a major change for you in that rules for decision-making and standards would need to be set down.

At present you have quarterly board meetings and a quarterly statement of accounts. Your annual accounts are of course audited – although from past records they are not finalised until six months after the year end. Your board agendas have in the past been administrative and mechanistic; there is no evidence of big decisions being taken there. Your annual budgeting process is thorough and clearly sets out the expected results for the year ahead. This, of course, is required by your bank who are closely monitoring forward and past performance.

My *key recommendations* to you about your board, of which you are a member, are as follows:

1. *Board of Directors*

   Select a non-executive chairman as your first step who has a good City reputation and who is prepared to give you the approximate three days a month you need. You would be best to use a search recruitment consultant for this. Once you have chosen as chair someone likely to be acceptable to investors and with whom you feel you can work, you can together select two non-executive directors who will bring a blend of skills.

   The board should meet eight or nine times per annum and you will need to agree items that are specifically reserved for the board's decision. I would expect that the new chairman will set out terms of reference for the board and will wish to agree with you how the two of you can best work together. At the end of each year the board will wish to review its own workings in an appraisal session so that areas of improvement can be identified. The non-executive directors should also form an audit committee and a remuneration committee.

2. *Information for all Directors*

   You will need to prepare monthly management accounts and to provide information that will enable the directors to really monitor the business against pre-determined plans. In my view, the following information should be available to all directors:

   - an annual presentation of the strategic plan for the three or five years ahead for the company;
   - the annual budget;
   - financial information on a monthly basis that shows profit and loss, cash flow and balance sheet information. This should show comparisons against budget and last year for the current month and the year to date; and the current forecast for the financial year compared with budget and last year;
   - management comments on the financial data above and the prognosis for the next (say, three) months ahead;

- a review of the key non-accounting measures that illustrate the health of your business, e.g.

  - plant utilisation – current and future expectations;
  - ratio of orders received to invoices raised in the current month;
  - labour and productivity measures;
  - material utilisation.

- key media articles on the company, the industry and especially the competition;
- analysts' reports on the company and its competitors;
- consumer satisfaction surveys and employee attitude surveys.

3. *Commitment to Communicate*

   You and your finance director will need to make a serious investment of time in communicating with the City. This will most naturally happen at the half year and full year when together you will present your results in more depth than would normally be included in statutory accounts. Your annual report will also be a window on your company and will need to be deeply informative and presented in an interesting, easy to read way. I repeat that this requires a commitment of your time. It is important to have high confidence in the company to ensure an appropriately valued share price at the beginning of the process. I expect that with your chosen broker you will need to go around the major institutions and sector analysts to present the strategy and past achievements of Barnes Engineering.

4. *Meetings of Non-executive Directors*

   The Chairman may wish to have an occasional meeting alone with non-executive directors to ensure that they are satisfied with the way the board is run, with the progress of the company and with the information they receive. This is normal. Given your unique position I certainly believe that you should join in these meetings although you should be prepared to absent yourself should circumstances suggest this as appropriate.

A key role of the chairman and of the non-executive directors is to monitor the chief executive and his executive team. You will need to formalise an appraisal process and be prepared to objectively review your own performance against predetermined objectives. This is in fact both helpful and positive for the executives concerned as well as the board itself. It should also be coupled to a succession plan for your top cadre of executives and yourself. The board will want to be satisfied that, in the next five years when you plan to give up your chief executive's role, succession plans are firmly in place and that the result is satisfactory.

5. *Review of Financial Procedures*
   Your finance director is experienced and capable. He should review your current financial controls to ensure that they are in keeping with best practice of a publicly quoted company – in particular, the evaluation of authority levels and of the segregation of duties to ensure that controls are satisfactory. I am also sure that any audit committee will require that a review of business risks is undertaken to satisfy themselves about the management controls.

This may sound a daunting list to you. It is fairly complete. Some people would see this as negative or time-consuming, but it is a necessary evil if you are going to go from private ownership to public. It can be seen as a set of rules that need to be complied with. However, my past experience and current belief is that this effort of improving standards of governance lifts professional standards in the company and can add value to an enterprise. Viewed from the outside, at least with appropriate standards laid down and with a board of like minded people who pay attention to the spirit of governance, then you can have much more confidence that at least value is not being lost due to inappropriate standards. Putting this in place is very important but you will need to ensure that you also communicate these standards to the market.

Best wishes for your proposed float of Barnes Engineering and for the new, exciting era ahead of you.

developed a little later. To summarise, we note that our research highlights:

1. The importance of relationships between the company's management and their shareholders.
2. Institutions do not wish to interfere with management but there are a number of areas where they wish to have better information, for example, in the selection of new directors.
3. Communication with shareholders has improved in recent times but can be improved further. This calls for a professional plan as well as time and effort on the part of the company. We did, however, note that small or individual shareholders want to find a way to share in the early communication of additional company information. At present they feel a little left our and are 'poor cousins' to the institutions.
4. Non-executive directors are an important and potentially powerful influence for good governance. They are currently under-exploited, under-trained, have insufficient time and need greater financial incentives in return for the contribution they can, and should, make.
5. The audit committee can provide greater assurance on good governance and financial matters. It should spend more time understanding and monitoring the risks faced by companies and not for profit organisations. It will need to review the control environment to ensure that this is adequate.
6. There is a need for greater transparency in company remuneration policy and in communicating the rewards of the directors. However, almost all shareholders want to see high rewards for the achievement of demanding targets of longer-term performance.
7. Almost universally, the research reinforced the view that the legislative or new code initiatives should be consolidated to allow good governance principles to become embedded in board practice without the distraction of new or altered rules.

The board and its evaluation

While it may seem simple to observe pragmatically that a board, like any top body, needs to have its goals and basic rules, we have seen plenty of examples where little or no thought has been directed to this concept. As a result, these bodies muddle along. We strongly hold the view that the board must agree how to manage itself and that it should formally appraise its own performance. The chairman should annually lead such a review of the body itself as well as discussing with individuals their performance against expectations. This, we believe, is simple, good practice.

The chairman has a key role and will need to show the required leadership skills to allow the different contributions and challenges, especially from non-executive directors, yet preserving team work and unity. While we do not believe that there is a universal solution to propose as the ideal board, we have taken time to think through the elements for the 'ideal' board which have been summarised in Figure 2.3.

The whole question of board evaluation is so important that we have broken this out as a separate chapter. Evaluation is a tool for improved corporate governance. We believe that:

- Performance evaluation of boards is vital to their long-term value-adding contributions.
- The current environment of rapid change and turbulence coupled with ever closer public scrutiny, with increased regulatory requirements, make the need for board evaluation greater than ever.
- The process of installing performance evaluation into board practice is unlikely to be easy. This needs to be recognised and patience exercised. There is evidence that simply imposing an evaluation process on directors as individuals could be disastrous for the board.
- The criteria for setting and assessing the objectivity of the evaluation process needs to be agreed and clearly understood in advance of implementation.
- Measuring progress against agreed standards is a fruitful exercise and is likely to lead to a continuous improvement in performance.
- Evaluation may well be an essential protective – as well as value-adding–corporate governance tool of the future.

The independent director and the investor

Business history shows that we have moved from the age of the entrepreneur who provides the capital, takes the risks and makes the decisions to an age where it is normal to separate capital from management. More latterly, we have seen in different western countries clear examples of shareholder activism. Today, there is a positive trend for institutional investors to engage actively with the board of companies in which they have a significant stake. For this reason we observed in

Chapter 4 that we have moved from entrepreneurial capitalism to managerial capitalism and now to shareholder capitalism.

A good deal of effort has been expended by large shareholders in recent times to persuade boards to think in terms of the efficient allocation of capital and the appropriateness of the asset base for producing agreed return on equity targets. Businesses that do not at least earn their weighted average cost of capital on new investments destroy shareholder value.

Relationship investing is a particularly popular variant of this shareholder activism. The relationship investor acquires a sizeable chunk of shares, takes a board seat and sets about giving advice aimed at lifting corporate performance over the medium term.

Major debate needs to occur on the breadth of the board's 'portfolio' or jurisdiction of influence. We believe it should include at least the following: monitoring the CEO's performance; ensuring legal compliance; ensuring ethical behaviour; signing off on the corporate strategy; monitoring strategy implementation.

We observe that an increasing number of boards are planning their composition with the firm's strategic goals in mind and are carrying out that planning by means of rigorous director selection procedures. This applies to the balance of the board drawn from executives or outside sources as non-executives. It also applies to the balance of skills and experience of the individuals who make up the board.

Dealing with the unexpected

Most directors do not warmly embrace an unexpected significant event such as a takeover bid for their company. It is time-consuming, creates new stresses and often drags the individuals into new areas where they feel impotent and unprepared. Yet there are some general principles that can be applied and companies can, to some extent, at least partially be prepared for the unexpected. There are five key messages that we have gleaned from the detail of Chapter 5:

1. Prior to any potential takeover activity, boards need to have asked the question 'Where might a raider look to improve value?' and to have taken appropriate action based on their answers to that question.
2. Boards need an agreed, documented course of action, with all parties identified, against the possibility of an unsolicited bid. A defence

manual is now the norm for most companies in economies where takeover activity is prevalent.

3. Anti-takeover devices are not in the interests of good corporate governance. Any controls should be enforced not by the board, but rather by the market in the form of sensible regulations.

4. Takeovers play a significant role in disciplining managerial performance and are an essential element in any solution to the problem of the separation of corporate ownership and control.

5. Tender offers and hostile takeovers are primary market mechanisms which encourage efficient management and competitive firms. Anti-takeover mechanisms subvert competition in the market for corporate control.

The control environment

Profitable, well-run companies do not shirk risk. They understand the various risks the enterprise faces, they understand the potential rewards measured against those risks and they allocate appropriate resource to ensure that satisfactory controls are in place. We have seen clear evidence that companies which have a clear understanding of the risks they face and which manage these in a satisfactory way will perform ahead of their peer group in the long run. Equally, we have seen that companies that take governance matters seriously will tend to be amongst the better-performing companies.

It is also clear from the evidence that we have gleaned that improvements in the control environment as well as governance in general will come more from exhortation and promulgating best practice than from increasing regulation or legislation.

Not-for-profit enterprises

Throughout this book there are many lessons, principles and observations made from a commercial company viewpoint but which are equally applicable to the not-for-profit sector. We did, however, feel that it was helpful to include Chapter 7 as a separate focus on this subject. There are four key points that we would like to highlight here:

1. There has been a dangerous tendency in this sector for directors with considerable management experience to compensate for the managerial vacuum in their organisations by becoming 'executives at one remove' and thus blurring the direction/management distinction.

2. A fundamental requirement for all voluntary associations is to understand that employees' administrative duties must be quite distinct from the boards' duty of direction.
3. Not-for-profit bodies should agree a board remit to serve as the foundation for its processes. This should go hand-in-hand with agreed principles defining the parameters of directors' true functions.
4. The key criteria in selecting directors for not-for-profit board should be: a capacity to understand and act in accordance with the peculiar stewardship requirements of this sector; to understand that the clients are the 'proprietors'; and to contribute to the setting of clear policy directions.

It will be readily seen that these principles are basic tenets of good practice that should be applied in the commercial area too.

Communication

Many people nod sagely in agreement with the often expressed view that communication is necessary in all aspects of management. However, the practice of communication is patchy at best and the disciplines for good practice and time investment needed are often lacking. Communication is fundamental in good governance and the ability to communicate is a fundamental prerequisite of the capable leader of any organisation. Lost opportunities in this area can be seen all around us today. The annual report is a case in point. A disciplined approach to communicating its key messages to various shareholders, as well as other stakeholders, is not always evident. The message must be tailor-made to a specific audience and then must be managed effectively. There is a continuing need for executive training in presentation and communication skills and this is not always recognised by the individuals concerned.

A model for consideration

Reflecting on the research, current thinking and the earlier chapters, we believe that there is a good case for moving forward by creating a new model that will form the basis of value creation and good governance in the years ahead. Before we propose the new model, let us review some salient common strands as the precursor.

Common strands

Throughout this book, and indeed in the writing of others who have studied the field of governance, there are some common strands. Grouping these together, we see the following:

- There is a need to align the interests of shareholders and professional management more closely.
- Company performance and potential returns to shareholders can be improved with genuine relationship investing where major stakes of more than 10 per cent but less than 20 per cent are taken and common goals agreed. Shareholders need to see themselves as owners and not just investors.
- Non-executive directors have a critical role to play. They need better training and more independence and need to be seen to be independent.
- The chairman's role and his or her performance is critical to the smooth, satisfactory working of the board.
- Proper evaluation procedures should be put in place so that the board is able to monitor its own effectiveness against agreed objectives.
- Shareholders should not be involved in the day-to-day running of the company. However, they need to be well informed through good, open communication so that they can come to a view about management's performance and the company's progress against well-understood goals. They also need to respect the principle that it is appropriate to have goals applicable to *all* shareholders only and that no special interest agenda is acceptable.
- Executive directors need to be well rewarded when they meet demanding targets, for without their motivation, their creativity, leadership and skills, the company will fall well short of optimum.

Improving the existing

There are those who argue that the current situation is 'unbroken' and does not require 'fixing'. So long as there is a vocal body of opinion that supports this view, its supporters will attempt to tweak up performance to be seen to be meeting some of the legitimate concerns of sections of society.

For example, on the question of remuneration, while present remuneration practice is broadly supported by institutions and individual shareholders, the case for improved disclosure would be universally supported. Take also the question of non-executive directors. Our survey shows that this is an area in which institutions felt that it would be helpful to consult them in advance of new appointments being made. They dislike voting down a proposal in public, other than in exceptional circumstances. Certainly, there was widespread support for abandoning cross-directorships, restricting the number of such appointments an individual can hold and even recognising in statute that a non-executive director's role and status *is* different from those of executive directors. There was also strong support for formal continuing training for directors and an induction programme for new ones.

Turning to a different area, the respondents in our study were clear, as we are, that the audit committee can make a greater value adding contribution. More than three-quarters were in favour of widening the scope and depth of the audit committee to require it to have a more proactive role, especially in areas of internal control and risk assessment and in understanding the balancing of risk with the available returns.

Improved communication between the management of a company and its shareholders will strengthen understanding and, we would argue, long-term performance. Institutions in particular felt that the top 20 shareholders should be consulted on matters such as:

	% of replies agreeing
• remuneration programmes for directors	67%
• significant strategy changes	50%
• board changes	47%

This ignores the smaller shareholders who, as we have highlighted in Chapter 1, also wish to have the same level of information and consultation as institutions. While their aspiration is understandable, it is not deliverable. Yet there are actions that can be taken to improve the quality of information to small and large shareholders alike. The annual general meeting is usually a missed opportunity while the letter from the chairman can be made more informative. Looking to the future, electronic messaging using the Internet to pass on information to shareholders will also grow.

Improvements can, and will, be made and there are few people who want more review bodies or legislative initiatives at this time. 'Let the present system settle down and get the good practice levels notched a little higher' is the greatest cry that we have heard. However, looking to the future, we believe there is merit in a new model that is more comprehensive and that will lift economic performance with a strong focus on long-term value creation and more congruence between owners and managers.

Proposed new model

Within the United Kingdom the top 50 institutions control £400 billion of equity funds which we would estimate is 45 per cent of the total. We would like to see them investing significantly in a relationship way with say up to 10 significant companies probably chosen from the FTSE 250 list. Their investments would need to be significant but not controlling and would be in the range of 10–19 per cent of the total equity. Recognising that the average duration of institutions' own liabilities is long term they should be prepared to invest for between five and ten years. This ties in neatly with the current eight years which the National Association of Pension Funds claims is the average holding period for any given share in a pension fund portfolio.

The boards of directors of these companies would move in balance to be weighted more towards non-executive directors. The chief executive and finance directors would be there in all cases but the practice of appointing other senior line executives would diminish over time. Clearly, the balance of the board will vary according to the company. Some will have additional executive directors from functions such as human resources, strategy or information systems while others will include two or three from major business areas where these executives have the breadth and ability to focus on issues from a company-wide view. Ideally, the board should not be more than twelve and have a majority of non-executive directors.

Non-executive directors would be nominated by the institutions perhaps on the basis of one director for each complete 10 per cent of their shareholding. They would also agree to add additional non-executive directors from an approved list of professionals who met the criteria agreed by shareholder bodies including institutions and ProShare. A new class of professional director would evolve who would be available to be appointed to appropriate companies from a register kept by a body such as the Institute of Directors. These would be highly experienced, professional people with specialist qualifications and a variety of rich experiences who would treat this as their main professional role. Certainly, they should be capable of undertaking up to five such appointments or one chairmanship and three such appointments so long as they had no executive roles elsewhere. Their selection would *not* be made by the executive directors although it would be sensible to have the chief executive involved in the final choice so as to reduce the possibility that chemistry issues do not arise later.

In total, it would be common for a board of such a company to have twelve directors, eight non-executive (two of whom are directly appointed by institutions with a qualifying ownership and the balance from the register) with the remainder executive directors. The chair, who would usually be part-time and independent, must have the charisma and capacity to make the board a productive body despite the possibility of divisions between the two groups of directors who would be separately recognised in law. This has already been done in Australia for example where there is seen to be merit in recognising in statute the differences in roles of executives and non-executives as well as agreeing areas of common responsibility. This is shown diagrammatically in Figure 9.2. We accept that given the present configuration of boards which typically have a majority of executive directors, this suggested target may take some time to achieve.

At the outset of such a new relationship forming, the non-executives would spend sufficient time with the management to understand deeply the key factors to help them come to a judgement about a long-term strategic plan. A 'contract' would be drawn up between the management and the board which would embody the strategy and list the key milestones and financial expectations. Either the institutions who are part

---

(Board size, say 12 maximum)

- Chairman (usually not executive).
- CEO and Finance Director and up to two additional executive directors. Over time, executive numbers are likely to reduce.
- Non-executive Directors nominated directly by institutions (one for each 10 per cent shareholding, say two).
- Non-executive Directors nominated from an approved list of professionals, say six.

Figure 9.2 Composition of board

owners need to be created insiders or preferably the key elements will need to be communicated to the Stock Exchange and all shareholders. This five-year plan becomes the basis by which progress is judged and upon which rewards are paid. Naturally enough, the plan will be updated over time and fine-tuned, for a plan is a living document, rather than a tablet of stone.

A board constructed in this way would then be in a much improved position to monitor management, especially the chief executive, as well as the overall progress of the company. The better qualified, patently independent, non-executive directors would form the audit and remuneration committees. Credibility should be high.

Executive directors' remuneration would be much more weighted to the longer term and achievement of the five-year plan. Although there may be a need for sensitive phasing in, we would expect to see base salaries reduced by about 25 per cent on average. Annual bonuses would be a maximum of 25 per cent for achieving agreed personal goals that would be clearly set down in advance, monitored and judged by the remuneration committee. The long-term incentive would be paid over the five-year achievement with a maximum payout when really stretching targets are achieved of five times average salary over that time. Then, a portion (probably a half) should be paid in shares in the company which would need to be held for two more years. Given pension requirements and the reduction in salary, consideration would need to be made to use some of this bonus to be deferred either as additional voluntary contributions (AVCs) or money purchase schemes. In any event, the companies will move more towards current payments from deferred, which is of course the American pattern.

Each company director, whether executive or non-executive, would be encouraged or even required to invest one year's income in the company in which he or she is a director. A programme to achieve this over a reasonable period can be agreed with the remuneration committee.

Benefits of new model

We believe there are significant benefits from the implementation of the model outlined above. In summary form these are:

- a closer bonding of owners and managers to commonly agreed, well-understood goals
- a focus on the strategic and longer term

- an opportunity for institutions to release potential value together with management and to make judgements about investments that create value for their constituent members
- an improved ability to monitor the business progress and the executive top team
- higher quality, non-executive directors who are better informed, more prepared to spend the appropriate time and who will be paid appropriately as any other professional adviser
- greater reassurance to society and other stakeholders of the integrity, checks and balances in the corporate world
- objectively set, high potential rewards for outstanding performance from the top management team.

Support for the new model

We would claim that there is a prima facie case of significant potential support for this model. It would meet Michael Porter's criteria set out in the research report of the Council of Competitiveness, *Capital Choices*, where he observed that 'the long-term interests of companies would be better served by having a smaller number of long-term or new permanent owners whose goals are better aligned with those of the corporation'.

Some major investors such as Warren Buffet already practise the relationship investment approach through their investment vehicles. The above average growth in value that they achieve pays testament to such an approach. The model achieves congruity between the aims of the owners and the aims of the managers. Our requirement that all directors, whether they are executive or non-executive, should build up an interest in the equity of the business that is equal to approximately one year's income provides such a solution. Certainly, Robert Galvin's investment of about $500m which is about 2 per cent of the value of Motorola puts him firmly in tune with shareholder interests. Motorola is an example of a class company with a class performance.

Closer to home, our model should logically find broad support from the Institute of Directors and there is a similarity between our proposals and the suggestions made by Allen Sykes at the Institute of Directors conference. Their record of proceedings highlights some significant observations as a precursor to Sykes's positive suggestions. First, it is observed that individual shareholders in the United Kingdom are virtually powerless in corporate governance. Second, that although institutions with 70 per cent of broad corporate ownership in the United

Kingdom have potential power, they do not exercise it. They are largely passive. However, as they are judged in their performance by *their* ultimate owners, they do buy and sell shares freely. Long-term relationships – as opposed to long-term investing – are in truth, quite rare.

Our model does address each of these issues. Individual shareholders will have an opportunity to be more involved through the nominations of directors as we have described above. Institutions will move to much greater involvement and long-term commitment. In those cases where management fail to live up to their promises, the representatives of the shareholders will more easily remove them.

Allen Sykes proposes a solution of which the key attributes are empathetic to our model. He would see 60 major institutions owning between 10 and 20 per cent of companies where five truly independent non-executive directors are appointed, not by the executive directors, but by the shareholders. These independent directors would act on the committees, negotiate with management a five-year plan and monitor the company's progress against this. There would be high rewards for outstanding performance based on the pattern used for venture capital buyouts. The independent directors would have access to the management, to all information at all times.

Sykes claims that no generally successful corporate governance system, either past or present, can exist without three ingredients: first, knowledgeable and committed long-term owners; second, management that is focused on and rewarded for long-term performance; finally, those managements must be held properly accountable to the vision that has been previously agreed. We concur with this view wholeheartedly.

General conclusion

There is a relatively good standard of governance already in place in most developed economies in the western world. Standards of good governance have evolved through the spread of best practice arising from compliance with the raft of regulations in recent years. However, we have observed, as have others before us, that companies with winning ways in good governance have tended to outperform their peer group. Looking from a more negative viewpoint, those companies who have installed adequate controls and which have a culture of high standards are less likely to fall through sudden collapse or malpractice.

In addition to searching out areas where improvements in governance can be made or in sharing best practice, we have also tried to make a number of suggestions that go beyond compliance; they seek to improve value and understanding as well as to reinforce the legitimacy of commercial enterprises as an essential element of society. Finally, we have suggested for the readers' consideration a new model that is feasible and value-adding but requires fundamental change on boards of directors and in institutions investing policies. Only time will tell whether the different sections have the courage to grasp the opportunities this provides.

Appendix I: Questionnaire to Institutions on Good Governance

1. In general, how would you best describe the
   central thrust of your investment policy?   Tick appropriate box

   - short term trading to maximise total return   ☐
   - buying or selling based on current relative value   ☐
   - medium term outlook   ☐
   - long term based on fundamental analysis   ☐
   - view of current management ability   ☐
   - attractiveness of strategy   ☐

2. Are you satisfied with the frequency and quality of
   company communication with the city?   Yes   No

   - frequency   ☐   ☐
   - quality   ☐   ☐   ☐

3. Do you think the institutions have an appropriate
   opportunity to influence companies on matters such
   as:-   Yes   No

   - strategy   ☐   ☐
   - management performance   ☐   ☐
   - appointment of new directors   ☐   ☐

   What suggestions do you have to improve the status
   quo?

   ....

   ....

   ....

   ....

   ....

4. In general, is the contribution from non-executives of
    a sufficiently high level to meet your expectations of
    good governance?   Yes   No

                                                             ☐   ☐

    If No, please give some ideas on how to improve.

    ....

    ....

    ....

    ....

    ....

5. Which (if any) of the following innovations to
    improve governance would you support?   Yes   No

    –   Creation of professional non-executive appointed
        by the top 20 shareholders of a company   ☐   ☐

    –   Abondoning cross board appointments of non-
        executive directors (i.e. where a company's direc-
        tors sit on colleague directors' boards)   ☐   ☐

    –   Restricting non-executive director appointments to
        three for a director who also has executive
        responsiblities and to six in other cases   ☐   ☐

    –   Recognising in statute that non-executive directors
        have a dual role as a legal director and to provide
        checks and balances on the executive   ☐   ☐

    –   Widening the scope and depth of the audit
        committee to require them to have a more proactive
        role, especially on matters of internal control,
        balancing risk and return   ☐   ☐

    –   Compulsory training for all directors to a minimum
        level including a period of orientation for new
        companies and "top-up" training of, say, 5 hours a
        year for all   ☐   ☐

    –   Required consultation by management with the top
        20 shareholders on matters such as:-

        –   significant changes to strategy   ☐   ☐
        –   changes to the board   ☐   ☐
        –   remuneration programmes for directors   ☐   ☐

    –   Rotating audit firms that audit the company every,
        say, 4 years   ☐   ☐

6. Which aspect of board-shareholder relations is most
    in need of improvement?

    ....
    ....
    ....
    ....
    ....

7. Do you have any suggestions to improve good
    governance and to grow closer relations between
    management and shareholders?

    ....
    ....
    ....
    ....
    ....

Thank you very much for your help.

Please post to:-

Prof David Band
Dean
Faculty of Business
Leeds Metropolitan University
80 Woodhouse lane
Leeds
LS2 8AB

All replies will be treated confidentially. If you would like a free summary report of
the findings please list your name and address below.

....
....
....
....
....

Appendix II: The Cadbury Code of Best Practice

THE CODE OF BEST PRACTICE

1 The Board of Directors

1.1 The board should meet regularly, retain full and effective control over the company and monitor the executive managements.

1.2 There should be a clearly accepted division of responsibilities at the head of a company, which will ensure a balance of power and authority, such that no one individual has unfettered powers of decision. Where the chairman is also the chief executive, it is essential that there should be a strong and independent element on the board, with a recognised senior member.

1.3 The board should include non-executive directors of sufficient calibre and number for their views to carry significant weight in the board's decisions. (Note 1)

1.4 The board should have a formal schedule of matters specifically reserved to it for decision to ensure that the direction and control of the company is firmly in its hands. (Note 2)

1.5 There should be an agreed procedure for directors in the furtherance of their duties to take independent professional advice if necessary, at the company's expense. (Note 3)

1.6 All directors should have access to the advice and services of the company secretary, who is responsible to the board for ensuring that board procedures are followed and that applicable rules and regulations are complied with. Any question of the removal of the company secretary should be a matter for the board as a whole.

2 Non-Executive Directors

2.1 Non-executive directors should bring an independent judgement to bear on issues of strategy, performance, resources, including key appointments, and standards of conduct.

2.2 The majority should be independent of management and free from any business or other relationship which could materially interfere with the exercise of their independent judgement, apart from their fees and shareholding. Their fees should reflect the time which they commit to the company. (Notes 4 and 5)

2.3   Non-executive directors should be appointed for specified terms and reappointment should not be automatic. (Note 6)

2.4   Non-executive directors should be selected through a formal process and both this process and their appointment should be a matter for the board as a whole. (Note 7)

3   Executive Directors

3.1   Directors' service contracts should not exceed three years without shareholders' approval. (Note 8)

3.2   There should be full and clear disclosure of directors' total emoluments and those of the chairman and highest-paid UK director, including pension contributions and stock options. Separate figures should be given for salary and performance-related elements and the basis on which performance is measured should be explained.

3.3   Executive directors' pay should be subject to the recommendations of a remuneration committee made up wholly or mainly of non-executive directors. (Note 9)

4   Reporting and Controls

4.1   It is the board's duty to present a balanced and understandable assessment of the company's position. (Note 10)

4.2   The board should ensure that an objective and professional relationship is maintained with the auditors.

4.3   The board should establish an audit committee of at least 3 non-executive directors with written terms of reference which deal clearly with its authority and duties. (Note 11)

4.4   The directors should explain their responsibility for preparing the accounts next to a statement by the auditors about their reporting responsibilities. (Note 12)

4.5   The directors should report on the effectiveness of the company's system of internal control. (Note 13)

4.6   The directors should report that the business is a going concern, with supporting assumptions or qualifications as necessary. (Note 13)

Appendix III: Greenbury Recommendations

2 CODE OF BEST PRACTICE

Introduction

2.1 The purpose of the accompanying Code is to set out best practice in determining and accounting for Directors' remuneration. The references at the end of each provision of the Code are to the fuller discussion in sections 4 to 7.

2.2 The detailed provisions have been prepared with large companies mainly in mind, but the principles apply equally to smaller companies.

2.3 We recommend that all listed companies registered in the UK should comply with the Code to the fullest extent practicable and include a statement about their compliance in the annual reports to shareholders by their remuneration committees or elsewhere in their annual reports and accounts. Any areas of non-compliance should be explained and justified.

2.4 We further recommend that the London Stock Exchange should introduce the following continuing obligations for listed companies:

- an obligation to include in their annual remuneration committee reports to shareholders or their annual reports a general statement about their compliance with section A of the Code which should also explain and justify any areas of non-compliance;

- a specific obligation to comply with the provisions in section B of the Code which are not already covered by existing obligations, and with provision C10 of the Code, subject to any changes fo working which may be desirable for legal or technical reasons.

2.5 Within section B, provision B3 requires remuneration committees to confirm that full consideration has been given to sections C and D of the Code.

THE CODE

A   **The remuneration committee**

A1   To avoid potential conflicts of interest, Boards of Directors should set up remuneration committees of Non-Executive Directors to determine on their behalf, and on behalf of the shareholders, within agreed terms of reference, the company's policy on executive remuneration and specific remuneration

Appendix III

packages for each of the Executive Directors, including pension rights and any compensation payments (paragraphs 4.3 – 4.7).

A2   Remuneration committee Chairmen should account directly to the shareholders through the means specified in this Code for the decisions their committees reach (paragraph 4.4).

A3   Where necessary, companies' Articles of Association should be amended to enable remuneration committees to discharge these functions on behalf of the Board (paragraph 4.3)

A4   Remuneration committees should consist exclusively of Non-Executive Directors with no personal financial interest other than as shareholders in the matters to be decided, no potential conflicts of interest arising from cross-directorships and no day-to-day involvement in running the business (paragraphs 4.8 and 4.11).

A5   The members of the remuneration committee should be listed each year in the committee's report to shareholders (B1 below). When they stand for re-election, the proxy cards should indicate their membership of the committee (paragraphs 4.12 and 5.25).

A6   The Board itself should determine the remuneration of the Non-Executive Directors, including members of the remuneration committee, within the limits set in the Articles of Association (paragraph 4.13).

A7   Remuneration committees should consult the company Chairman and/or Chief Executive about their proposals and have access to professional advice inside and outside the company (paragraph 4.14 – 4.17).

A8   The remuneration committee Chairman should attend the company's Annual General Meeting (AGM) to answer shareholders' questions about Directors' remuneration and should ensure that the company maintains contact as required with its principal shareholders about remuneration in the same way as for other matters (paragraph 5.27).

A9   The committee's annual report to shareholders (B1 below) should not be a standard item of agenda for AGMs. But the committee should consider each year whether the circumstances are such that the AGM should be invited to approve the policy set out in their report and should minute their conclusions (paragraphs 5.28 – 5.32).

B   Disclosure and approval provisions

B1   The remuneration committee should make a report each year to the shareholders on behalf of the Board. The report should form part of, or be annexed to, the company's Annual Report and Accounts. It should be the main vehicle through which the company accounts to shareholders for Directors' remuneration (paragraph 5.4).

B2   The report should set out the Company's policy on executive remuneration, including levels, comparator groups of companies, individual components, performance criteria and measurement, pension provision, contracts of service and compensation commitments on early termination (paragraphs 5.5 – 5.7).

B3 The report should state that, in framing its remuneration policy, the committee has given full consideration to the best practice provisions set out in sections C and D below (paragraph 5.25).

B4 The report should also include full details of all elements in the remuneration package of each individual Director by name, such as basic salary, benefits in kind, annual bonuses and long-term incentive schemes including share options (paragraphs 5.8 – 5.12).

B5 Information on share options, including SAYE options, should be given for each Director in accordance with the recommendations of the Accounting Standards Board's Urgent Issues Task Force Abstract 10 and its successors (paragraphs 5.13 – 5.16).

B6 If grants under executive share option or other long-term incentive schemes are awarded in one large block rather than phased, the report should explain and justify (paragraph 6.29).

B7 Also included in the report should be pension entitlements earned by each individual Director during the year, calculated on a basis to be recommended by the Faculty of Actuaries and the Institute of Actuaries (paragraphs 5.17 – 5.23).

B8 If annual bonuses or benefits in kind are pensionable the report should explain and justify (paragraph 6.44).

B9 The amounts received by, and commitments made to, each Director under B4, B5 and B7 should be subject to audit (paragraph 5.4).

B10 Any service contracts which provide for, or imply, notice periods in excess of one year (or any provisions for predetermined compensation on termination which exceed one year's salary and benefits) should be disclosed and the reasons for the longer notice periods explained (paragraph 7.13).

B11 Shareholdings and other relevant business interests and activities of the Directors should continue to be disclosed as required in the Companies Acts and London Stock Exchange Listing Rules (paragraph 5.24).

B12 Shareholders should be invited specifically to approve all new long-term incentive schemes (including share option schemes) whether payable in cash or shares in which Directors or senior executives will participate which potentially commit shareholders' funds over more than one year or dilute the equity (paragraph 5.33).

C **Remuneration policy**

C1 Remuneration committees must provide the packages needed to attract, retain and motivate Directors of the quality required but should avoid paying more than is necessary for this purpose (paragraphs 6.5 – 6.7).

C2   Remuneration committees should judge where to position their company relative to other companies. They should be aware what other comparable companies are paying and should take account of relative performance (paragraphs 6.11 – 6.12).

C3   Remuneration committees should be sensitive to the wider scene, including pay and employment conditions elsewhere in the company, especially when determining annual salary increases (paragraph 6.13).

C4   The performance-related elements of remuneration should be designed to align the interests of Directors and shareholders and to give Directors keen incentives to perform at the highest levels (paragraph 6.16).

C5   Remuneration committees should consider whether their Directors should be eligible for annual bonuses. If so, performance conditions should be relevant, stretching and designed to enhance the business. Upper limits should always be considered. There may be a case for part-payment in shares to be held for a significant period (paragraphs 6.19 – 6.22).

C6   Remuneration committees should consider whether their Directors should be eligible for benefits under long-term incentive schemes. Traditional share option schemes should be weighed against other kinds of long-term incentive scheme. In normal circumstances, shares granted should not vest, and options should not be exercisable, in under three years. Directors should be encouraged to hold their shares for a further period after vesting or exercise subject to the need to finance any costs of acquisition and associated tax liability (paragraphs 6.23 – 6.34).

C7   Any new long-term incentive schemes which are proposed should preferably replace existing schemes or at least form part of a well-considered overall plan, incorporating existing schemes, which should be approved as a whole by shareholders. The total rewards potentially available should not be excessive (paragraph 6.35). (*See* also B12.)

C8   Grants under incentive schemes, including new grants under existing share option schemes, should be subject to challenging performance criteria reflecting the company's objectives. Consideration should be given to criteria which reflect the company's performance relative to a group of comparator companies in some key variables such as total shareholder return (paragraphs 6.38 – 6.40).

C9   Grants under executive share option and other long-term incentive schemes should normally be phased rather than awarded in one large block (paragraph 6.29). (*See* B6.)

C10   Executive share options should never be issued at a discount (paragraph 6.29).

C11   Remuneration committees should consider the pension consequences and associated costs to the company of basic salary increases, especially for Directors close to retirement (paragraphs 6.42 – 6.45).

C12   In general, neither annual bonuses nor benefits in kind should be pensionable (paragraph 6.44). (*See* B8.)

D **Service contracts and compensation**

D1 Remuneration committees should consider what compensation commitments their Directors' contracts of service, if any, would entail in the event of early termination, particularly for unsatisfactory performance (paragraph 7.10).

D2 There is a strong case for setting notice or contract periods at, or reducing them to, one year or less (*see* B10). Remuneration committees should, however, be sensitive and flexible, especially over timing. In some cases notice or contract periods of up to two years may be acceptable. Longer periods should be avoided wherever possible (paragraphs 7.11 – 7.15).

D3 If it is necessary to offer longer notice or contract periods, such as three years, to new Directors recruited from outside, such periods should reduce after the initial period (paragraph 7.16).

D4 Within the legal constraints, remuneration committees should tailor their approach in individual early termination cases to the wide variety of circumstances. The broad aim should be to avoid rewarding poor performance while dealing fairly with cases where departure is not due to poor performance (paragraphs 7.17 – 7.18).

D5 Remuneration committees should take a robust line on payment of compensation where performance has been unsatisfactory and on reducing compensation to reflect departing Directors' obligations to mitigate damages by earning money elsewhere (paragraphs 7.19 – 7.20).

D6 Where appropriate, and in particular where notice or contract periods exceed one year, companies should consider paying all or part of compensation in instalments rather than one lump sum and reducing or stopping payment when the former Director takes on new employment (paragraph 7.20).

References

Arthur Andersen, *Audit Committees after Cadbury*, 1993.

Arthur Andersen, *Boardroom Pay in the FTSE 250: A Framework for Remuneration Committees*, Arthur Andersen & Co., 1995.

Arthur Andersen, *Global Best Practices for Audit Committees* (undated).

Arthur Andersen, *Managing Business Risks: An Integrated Approach*, The Economist Intelligence Unit, 1995.

Bain, Neville, *Successful Management*, Macmillan, 1995.

Bennis, Warren, *An Invented Life*, Addison-Wesley Publishing Company, 1993.

Berle, A. A. and G. C. Means, *The Modern Corporation and Private Property*, (Transaction 1991).

Blair, Margaret, *Ownership and Control*, The Brookings Institution, 1995.

Boddy, D., *Managing Change in Changing Times*, Management Services, October 1993, pp. 22–7.

Bogan, C. E. and M. J. English, 'Benchmarking: A Wakeup Call for Board Members (and CEOs Too)', *Planning Review*, July/August 1993, pp. 28–33.

Bostock, Richard (unpublished paper delivered to the British Academy of Management's Conference) Sept. 1995.

Buchholtz, A. K. and B. A. Ribbens, 'Role of Chief Executive Officers in Takeover Resistance: Efforts of CEO Incentives and Individual Characteristics', *Academy of Management Journal*, June 1994, pp. 554–79.

Cadbury, Sir Adrian, 'Ethical Managers Make their Own Rules', *Harvard Business Review*, 65, September/October 1987.

Cadbury, Sir Adrian, 'Report of the Committee on the Financial Aspects of Corporate Governance', Dec. 1992.

Cadbury, Sir Adrian, *The Company Chairman*, Director Books, Simon Schuster International Group, 1990.

Canadian Institute of Chartered Accountants, *Governance Processes for Control*, November, 1995.

Charkham, Jonathon, *Keeping Good Company – A Study of Corporate Governance in Five Countries*, Oxford University Press, 1994.

Cleaver, Sir Anthony, *Tomorrow's Company: The Role of Business in a Changing World*, RSA, 1995.

Clinnard, Marshall B., *Corporate Corruption: The Abuse of Power*, Praeger, 1990.

Clutterbuck, David and Peter Waine, *The Independent Board Director: Selecting and Using the Best Non-executive Directors to Benefit your Business*, McGraw-Hill, 1994.

Coopers & Lybrand, *Effective Business Control: A Guide for Directors*, June 1993.

Crook, Clive, 'The Future of Capitalism', *The Economist*, 11 September, 1993.

Daily, C. M. and D. R. Dalton, 'Board of Directors Leadership and Structure: Control and Performance Implications', *Entrepreneurship: Theory and Practice*, Spring 1993, pp. 65–81.

Daniels, John L. and N. Caroline Daniels, *Global Visions: Building New Models for the Corporation of the Future*, McGraw-Hill, 1993.

Deane, R., 'Beseiged by Duties: Will the New Companies Act Work for Directors?', New Zealand Society of Accountants and New Zealand Law Society Company Law Conference, 1994.

Demb, Ada, and F. Friedrich Neubauer, *The Corporate Board – Confronting the Paradoxes*, Oxford University Press, 1992.

Donaldson, Gordon, 'A New Tool for Boards: The Strategic Audit', *Harvard Business Review*, July–August 1995.

Donaldson, Thomas, *Corporations and Morality*, Prentice-Hall, 1982.

Drucker, Peter F., *Managing the Future: The 1990s and Beyond*, Dutton, 1992.

Eccles, Robert G. and Sarah C. Maurinac, 'Improving the Corporate Disclosure Process', *Sloan Management Review*, Summer 1995.

Ernst & Young, *New Directions for Audit Committees*, 1992.

Ernst & Young, *Corporate Governance: Remuneration Disclosures*, 1995.

Everitt, Haydon and Martyn Jones, *The Audit Committee and its Chairman*, Touche Ross, 1992.

Financial Times, 'Small Investors Turn Up the Heat in France', 14 September 1995.

Fram, E. H. and R. F. Pearse, 'When Worse Comes to Worst: Terminating the Executive Director', *Nonprofit World*, November/December 1990, pp. 31–3.

Gardner, Howard, *Leading Minds: An Anatomy of Leadership*, HarperCollins, 1996.

Gordon, L. A. and J. Pound, 'The Challenge of Governing for Value', *Directors and Board*, Spring 1992, pp. 13–17.

Greenbury, Sir Richard, *Directors Remuneration; Report of a Study Group*, Gee Publishing, July 1995 (referred to as the Greenbury Report).

Handy, Charles, *The Age of Unreason*, Business Books Limited, 1989.

Handy, Charles, *The Empty Raincoat*, Hutchinson, 1994.

Harvey-Jones, John, *Making it Happen*, Collins, 1988.

Hay Group, *Boardroom Remuneration Review: Is Executive Remuneration Working?*, Summer 1995.

Hind, Andrew, *The Governance and Management of Charities*, Voluntary Sector Press, 1996.

Hussey, Prof. Roger, *Shareholders Questions at the AGM*, Touche Ross, November 1995.

Institute of Directors, *Enterprise and Governance – The Proceedings of a Conference held at the Institute of Directors*, 24 October 1995.

Jensen, Michael C., 'Eclipse of the Public Corporation', *Harvard Business Review*, 67, September/October 1989.

Kesner, I. F. and D. R. Dalton, 'Anti-Takeover Tactics: Management 42 Stocktakers 0', *Business Horizon*, October 1985, pp. 17–25.

Leighton, D. S. R. and D. H. Thain, 'Selecting New Directors', *Business Quarterly*, Summer 1993, pp. 17–25.

Leighton, D. S. R. and D. H. Thain, *Improving Board Effectiveness: The Role of the Chairman*, Corporate Governance, Western Business School, University of Western Ontario, 1993.

Leighton, D. S. R. and D. H. Thain, *The Director's Dilemma: What's My Job?*, Corporate Governance, Western Business School, University of Western Ontario, 1993.

Lev, B., 'Information Disclosure Strategy', *California Management Review*, Summer 1992, pp. 9–32.

Lindsell, D., 'Blueprint for an Effective Audit Committee', *Accountancy*, vol. 110, December 1992.

Lorsch, J. W., *Pawns or Potentates*, Harvard Business School Press, 1989.

Lusch, R. F. and M. G. Harvey, 'The Case for an Off-Balance-Sheet Controller', *Sloan Management Review*, Winter 1994, pp 101–5.

Mallette, P. and K. L. Fowler, 'Effects of Board Composition and Stock Ownership on the Adoption of 'Poison Pills', *Academy of Management Journal*, 35 (1992), pp. 1010–1035.

Mercer, William, *Survey of the Institutional Investors on the Greenbury Report*, September, 1995.

Michaels, M., 'CEO Evaluation: The Board's Second Most Crucial Duty', *Nonprofit World*, May/June 1990, pp. 29–32.

Mohn, Reinhard, *Success through Partnerships*, Bantam, 1989.

Monks, Robert A. G. and Nell Minow, *Corporate Governance*, Blackwell Business, 1995.

Mueller, R. K., 'A Director's Performance Appraisal', *Directors and Boards*, Spring 1993, pp. 16–27.

National Association of Corporate Directors, *Performance Evaluation of Chief Executive Officers, Boards and Directors*, NACD, 1994.

New Bridge Consultants, 'UK Top 500 Companies Board Rewards Survey', September 1995.

Nichol, R. I., 'Get Middle Managers Involved in the Planning Process', *Journal of Business Strategy*, 1993.

Ozaki, Robert S., *Human Capitalism*, Penguin, 1991.

Parker, Hugh, 'The Company Chairman – His Role and Responsibilities', *Long Range Planning*, 23 April 1990.

Parker, Hugh, *Letter to a New Chairman*, 2nd edn, Director Books, 1989.

Plender, John, 'The Great Fudge of Cadbury', *Financial Times*, 4 July 1995.

Porter, Michael, E., *Capital Choices: Changing the Way America Invests in Industry, Research Report of the Council on Competitiveness*, co-sponsored by the Harvard Business School, June 1992.

Price Waterhouse, *Improving Audit Committee Performance: What Works Best*, The Institute of Internal Auditors Research Foundation, 1993.

Rechner, P. L., 'Corporate Government: Fact or Fiction?', *Business Horizon*, vol. 32, no. 4, 1989, pp. 11–15.

Rechner, P. L. and D. R. Dalton, 'CEO Duality as Organizational Performer: A Longitudinal Analysis', *Strategic Management Journal*, 12, 1991, pp. 155–60.

Russell Reynolds Associates, 'Independent Directors: UK Companies', 1995 250 Survey, 1995.

Salmon, W. J., 'Crisis Prevention: How to Gear Up Your Board', *Harvard Business Review*, January/February 1993, pp. 68–75.

Saxton Bamphylde International, *Non-Executive Directors*, June 1995.

Scott, R. M., 'Total Quality Management in Education', Winston Churchill Memorial Trust Board, Wellington 1993.

Semler, Ricardo, *Maverick: The Story Behind the World's Most Unusual Work Place*, Warner Books, 1993.

Spencer Stuart, *Pay at the Top*, Spencer Stuart & Associates Limited, 1994.

Sykes, Allen, 'Proposals for Internationally Competitive Corporate Governance in Britain and America', *Corporate Governance: An International Review, 2, 3*, 1994, pp. 187–95.

Touche Ross, 'The Financial Aspects of Corporate Governance', Progress Report No. 8, November 1995.

Treadway Commission, *The Committee of Sponsoring Organisations of the Treadway Commission Report*, September 1992.

Useem, M., *Executive Defense: Shareholder Power and Corporate Reorganization*, Harvard University Press, 1993.

Vitale, M., S. Maurinac and M. Hauser, 'New Process/Financial Scorecard: A Strategic Performance Measurement System', *Planning Review*, July-August 1994, pp. 12–16.

Zander, A., *Making Board Effective*, Jossey-Bass, 1993.

Index